CONCILIUM

CONCILIUM 2000/1

EVOLUTION AND FAITH

Edited by
Bas van Iersel (†), Christoph Theobald
and Hermann Häring

SCM Press · London

Published by SCM Press, 9–17 St Albans Place,
London N1

ISBN: 0 334 03057 9

Typeset by Regent Typesetting, London
Printed by Biddles, Ltd, Guildford and King's Lynn

Concilium Published February, April, June, October, December.

Contents

Introduction

Evolution and Faith

Along with the theory of relativity and psychoanalysis, the theory of evolution is one of the Western mega-theories of our time. In the nineteenth century it caused an epistemological revolution in biology and anthropology. In the twentieth century it was followed by cosmology and the behavioural sciences. Philosophy has long been reconciled to it. Faith and theology have found things more difficult. Granted, Western thought is stamped right through with the notion of evolution, but biblical ideas are still often seen as competition. Creationism still defends the traditional idea of a God who created human beings directly and then appointed them to rule the world. At the opposite extreme, some critics of religion still think that they can use the theory of evolution to prove that the notion of creation is absurd. A third group of theologians and scientists is basically uninterested in the question. For them science and faith have nothing to say to each other; they live in two worlds. The present issue will be primarily concerned with this group.

Do faith and the theory of evolution really have nothing to say to each other? It is legitimate to doubt this, for ideas of life and the cosmos have been fundamentally changed by the theory of evolution. We no longer argue over whether or not Darwin was right. Rather, we want to know what the theory of evolution means for faith and theology today. What does this new vision mean for a believing understanding of the cosmos, life and humankind? How can we differentiate it from earlier and outdated oppositions between faith and science? If theology is prepared to learn from this new world view it can also formulate its critical questions more credibly. How can the instrumental biologism of a technological world effectively be replaced by a real reverence for life? How can the theory of evolution be protected from being misused for a naïve and arrogant notion of progress? Must not the inexorable survival of the fittest be opposed by the central biblical message of mercy towards the weak?

Even while we were preparing this issue we were aware that it would involve treading the narrow line between specialist knowledge and a more widely understandable account. Here the concept of evolution itself presented the fewest problems. 'Evolution' today is understood to mean the overall development of life – so to speak from the first cell to the present multiplicity. Here the emphasis is on the conviction that we can really speak of a single process of evolution. Certainly there can be slower and quicker developments in this evolution, even 'leaps' and qualitative changes; theorists may argue over their precise analysis and explanation. But the theory of evolution maintains that the whole of life is to be understood as a single process. Granted, many theoreticians do not exclude the possibility that one can also talk of the action of God in this development, but they will never accept that God intervenes at particular points, appears so to speak as a cause and thus determines the course of evolution from the outside. There may perhaps be a dispute as to when and how this process of evolution begins, for the analyses of the beginning, the first forms and the pre-forms of life will become increasingly differentiated. But at this point, too, there is increasing conviction that the first steps are also to be explained in terms of the self-organization of matter.

So is God being increasingly forced to the periphery? Or is God being understood more and more as an immanent principle that is always present? So does the miracle of life consist in the intervention by God in matter? Or is it not a still greater miracle that matter has the life-force in it from the beginning? Theologians have to answer those questions. They are caught in the tension between the biblical tradition and the scientific world-view. At the same time they must not forget that they themselves can think again about the concept of life. For God has always been understood as life, and in the Bible and tradition the great human utopia is constantly called life.

So it is important that in the first part of this issue we note the influence of the theory of evolution on contemporary culture. This is done in the articles by Bloemers and Häring. In the second part various aspects of the theory of evolution are studied at a deeper level. The notion of evolution embraces not only earthly life but the whole cosmos in a great comprehensive unity. How can this unity be described more closely (De Schrijver)? What criticism has creationism to make of the theory of evolution (Drees)? What does evolution look like from the perspective of Whitehead's process philosophy (Suchocki)? Finally, Christoph Theobald puts the concept of life in a broad religious and theological framework. The third part discusses concrete issues in the conversation with faith and theology. These include the Christian image of human beings (Michollet), the relationship between science and biblical discourse generally (Campbell), and quite specifically two different and contrasted messages, which van Iersel discovers in the theory of evolution and in the Bible. Comparisons with Teilhard de Chardin (Galleni) and Sri Aurobindo (Aykara) conclude this theme.

The theory of evolution is often associated with the harsh struggle for survival: the biblical message of concern for the disadvantaged is diametrically opposed to this principle. This notion was important above all to our colleague and friend Bas van Iersel, who died on 7 July 1999. He was instrumental in proposing the theme of this issue and strongly inspired its shape; it bears his mark. So in addition to his own article we have included two further articles which were written before his death and which first appeared – in collaboration with him – in the Dutch journal *Schrift*. These are the articles by P. Bloemers and W. B. Dress. We are grateful to Bas van Iersel for his work. In connection with his article this issue also contains a brief appreciation of him and his work for *Concilium*.

Hermann Häring and Christoph Theobald

I. The Theory of Evolution and Its Influence

A Modern Understanding of Life: The View of an Orthodox Evolutionist

PETER BLOEMERS

'For the fate of the sons of men and the fate of the beasts is the same; as one dies, so dies the other. They all have the same breath, and man has no advantage over the beasts. For all is vanity. All go to one place; all are from the dust, and all turn to dust again. Who knows whether the spirit of man goes upward and the spirit of the beast goes down to the earth?' (Ecclesiastes 3.19–21).

The rapid progress of the natural sciences in the last century and a half has thoroughly changed our view of the world. Important elements of the modern world-view have gradually become part of the intellectual baggage of people whose views were earlier governed above all by a quite literal interpretation of the Bible. It in fact seems as if this whole process has gone relatively calmly. But appearances are deceptive. Perhaps we have to say that natural scientists and (orthodox) Christians comfortably live separate lives. In so far as scientists are not atheists, in general they have a very abstract belief. They realize that what we perceive with our senses is an incomplete representation of reality and accept that those who set down the Bible in writing did so with a quite different representation of the same reality before their eyes. It is senseless to try to make these two representations agree.

On the other hand fundamentalists, of whatever faith, are a long way from scientists: consciously or unconsciously they have shut themselves off from the spectacular discoveries in astrology, physics, chemistry, geology and biology. Sometimes, however, it is impossible to avoid a harsh confrontation, and that provokes strong emotions from both sides.

Astronomy

Let's look more closely at the interaction between specific natural sciences and the church, or rather the absence of it. First astrology. This science enjoys the doubtful honour of having had the first serious clash with the magisterium. This was over the view of Copernicus that the sun and not the earth is the centre of our planetary system. Copernicus' work, which appeared in 1543, was put on the Index from 1611 to 1759. In 1633 the aged Galileo Galilei, a follower of Copernicus, was persecuted by the Inquisition for this view. Although it is only very recently that the Vatican has announced an official rehabilitation of Galileo, since the Enlightenment both the Catholic Church and most Protestant churches have had few problems with the fact that the earth is not the centre of the universe.

Present-day astronomy amazes us with theories which go far beyond our capacity for understanding: photons (particles of light) from the remotest corners of the universe which are fifteen billion years on the way before they reach our retinas, so that even today we are witnesses to the 'Big Bang', the creation of the universe. However, because such a photon is moving at the speed of light, according to the theory of relativity no time has passed at all, so that we have to say that while the 'Big Bang' took place fifteen billion years ago, it is still taking place today.

Astronomers have also come to the conclusion that the universe is not just unlimited, but also finite. It has a finite volume, just as a sphere has an unlimited but finite upper surface. Thus space is curved just like a sphere and in the fourth dimension has a curved radius, the length of which can be measured. In the universe things do not take place in the three-dimensional space of our world of experience, but in multi-dimensional space. How many dimensions? That is not a good question. Dimensions are only an expedient which scientists use in their attempt to describe nature.

There is a strong probability that in the universe there are 'black holes', so-called because the power of gravity in them is so strong that even the light cannot escape. Some astronomers think that these are tunnels of a higher dimension to other 'universes' outside our own. There is no point in trying to imagine what I have described here with inadequate words. But these vague pictures can inspire us to wonder at creation. For some Christians the time-scale, fifteen billion years, is unacceptable. Other problems arise from the current view among astronomers that intelligent life must have arisen at many places in the universe with its billions of galaxies, each with billions of stars.

However, many of these ideas and insights are unproven and largely unknown to the public. Almost nothing about them is taught at school and so far a new confrontation with fundamentalists has not materialized.

Physics

During evolution – to anticipate the story – our sense organs have become tuned to the things around us. We can see, hear and feel within a range from several kilometres to about a millimetre. By now our power of abstraction has become so great that we also understand what we see in a microscope or on a globe. However, the universe is far too great to comprehend with our mind, as I have already indicated. The world of modern physics is similarly far too small. Quantum mechanics is the theory of elementary particles, molecules, atoms and their many components. It teaches that matter and energy (two forms of the same thing) have the character of a wave; that the more precisely the position of a particle is determined, the more indeterminate the speed of that same particle is, and vice versa (Heisenberg's indeterminacy theory). Moreover particles and even whole systems can be in contradictory states. Erwin Schrödinger, a pioneer in this field, explained this with a story about a cat in a perilous position. The cat is put in a closed box. In this box there is an apparatus which is randomly made to give off a poison gas which will kill the cat. It is impossible to tell from the outside whether this has happened. Common sense tells us that the cat must either be dead or alive. If we open the box, we can see what the case is. However, quantum mechanics teaches that the cat is both alive and dead. If we open the box to look, then the cat is no longer in that peculiar state, but returns to one of the two states which we denote by 'living' and 'dead'. Thus the state of an object changes by perception. This seems to be a feeble play on words, but when used in connection with the behaviour of elementary particles, it is how quantum mechanics explains and predicts the 'illogical' properties of those particles. Here it forms the basis for modern physics, astrology and chemistry.

The apparently supernatural consequences to which quantum mechanics leads appeal to a feeling for mysticism, of the kind that one meets in new-age-like figures. A book has appeared, G. Zukav's *The Dancing Wu Li Masters*, in six parts, each of which is entitled Part One and each of which consists of a number of chapters, all of which are Chapter 1. In a fascinating way this book makes a link between physics and Taoism. However, both serious physicists, and also a serious Taoist whom I know, say that this is nonsense. Quantum mechanics is inaccessible to those who have not been initiated into it, and so is Taoism. Fortunately I have not heard attempts to explain Bible stories with quantum mechanics. That seems to me to be an impossible course to take.

Chemistry

The Bible does not say anything about the nature of matter. This fortunate, but by no means obvious, fact has probably spared chemists a clash with the church. Greek philosophers were, however, interested in matter, especially in the question whether one can divide matter into ever smaller fragments until one reaches infinity, or whether one must presuppose that there are smallest particles which cannot be divided further. This last view, put forward by Democritus (c.480–370 BC), fits in well with modern chemistry. In previous centuries indications of the existence of atoms and molecules accumulated, but until the beginning of the twentieth century there were chemists who recognized that it is useful to denote matter with chemical formulae, but who refused to accept that sugar, $C_{12}H_{22}O_{11}$, consists of molecules each of which is constructed of 12 atoms of carbon, 22 atoms of hydrogen and 11 atoms of oxygen.

All doubts have now disappeared. Quantum mechanics shows how the bond between atoms is made and broken in chemical reactions. On the basis of this knowledge a chemistry has developed which to a high degree influences our daily life. 'Chemistry is Everywhere' is the motto of the Royal Dutch Chemical Society, and indeed without chemistry the earth would not have the capacity to feed six billion people. We would never live to be as old and be as healthy as now (not even in the Third World), and our advanced technological development would never have come about. There is another side to the coin, but a conflict with biblical insights is not part of it.

Geology

With geology we do, however, get straight on to slippery ice. It is certain that the earth came into being around 4.6 billion years ago. Probably there was already unicellular life 800 million years later. The dating of rocks, and thus of fossils in them, can be determined with reasonable accuracy, above all in strata which are more recent than one billion years, the period in which multicellular plants and animals have developed. The geological periods (Quaternary, Tertiary, Cretaceous, Jurassic, etc.) fit on a clear time scale, giving a complete picture of the development of life on earth over the last 600 million years. It is certain that the dinosaurs, who have made a powerful impact on the public imagination, died out 60 million years ago. In contrast to what many children's books suggest, human beings and dinosaurs never had adventures together, since we only appeared on the scene between two and four million years ago (two or four, because that depends on what ape-like creatures one wants to begin to call man. There was no sharp transition).

At school I still learned that by chance Europe and Africa 'fit' into North and South America. Other continents, too, seem to be parts of a jigsaw puzzle. Inspired by these striking forms, in 1912 the German geologist Alfred Wegener put forward the theory that once all continents were joined together and formed one primal continent, Pangaea. At the time he found few supporters for this daring idea, but now the splitting and collision of continents, known as continental drift, is completely accepted. Furthermore, the indications are so numerous and fit together so well that it is thought possible roughly to map the shifting of the continental floes in the last 300 million years. Thus the Himalayas and the Alps are the result of recent collisions (45 million years ago) between Eurasia and the Indian subcontinent and Africa respectively. The places where earthquakes occur also coincide with faults which are the consequence of continental drift. We can also recognize the splitting up of continents in related fauna and flora, for example in the occurrence of koala bears in Australia and South America.

In general geologists are active far from home in the search for oil. Their discipline is not taught in schools. The wrath which the heterodoxy of biologists arouses among some of God's servants goes almost completely over their heads; we shall limit ourselves to their discoveries and views.

Biology

Of all the natural sciences biology is the least abstract. One does not need a mathematical training to be able to understand biology. It does not have the unimaginably large or unimaginably small as the object of its study, but precisely what we are most familiar with from our birth onwards, our fellow creatures, the plants and animals around us, and of course human beings. Like other natural science biology has a strong theoretical basis, in this case the theory of evolution. Without the theory of evolution, biology would lapse into a kid of philately, a postage-stamp collection of animals and planets.

Honesty compels me to say that the theory of evolution has a few weak points, which are constantly attacked by creationists in order to discredit it. Has the theory of evolution really been proved? No, but that is not the case with any scientific theory. However, the theory of evolution causes itself an extra difficulty. Following Popper, among others, we may require of a scientific theory that it is the simplest explanation of our perceptions and that it can be falsified. If a theory predicts that a particular phenomenon will occur in particular circumstances, then the scientist will devise an experiment in which these circumstances are imitated as well as possible, in order to see whether the phenomenon does then indeed take place. If that does not prove to be the case, the theory must be adapted or replaced by quite a different one. Unfortunately this does not work for some events. The origin of species (plants and animals) cannot be imitated and therefore a theory about their origin cannot be falsified.

A second weakness is the circular argument in which one gets caught up if one tries to support the theory of evolution with examples derived from the survival of the fittest (polar bears in the polar regions, giraffes in a landscape with tall trees). Survival of the fittest is an open door. Who is the fittest? Of course the one who survives. So it is not a matter of whether the best-adapted species survives. That would be the case even if Darwin were wrong. The question is whether the species indeed arose from one another in a way like that indicated by Darwin.

As for that, the indications that all life on earth arose from a primal cell are so comprehensive that among biologists, with some exceptions who have almost died out, there is no doubt about the fact. Note the way in which I have formulated this: *the origin of all life from one primal cell* and not *the theory that human beings are descended from apes*. The latter statement is indeed true, but relates to only one of the tens of millions of times that a new species has originated; in other words, that a population has developed for so long apart from its nearest kin that crossing between the two groups is no longer possible. The resistance which Darwin encountered was definitely not inspired only by the book of Genesis. However, it was a great shock to the arrogant Europeans that we really are a species of ape. I had thought that this fearful truth had by now slowly been assimilated, but during the recent commotion in The Netherlands about the doctrine of evolution in final school examinations, the letters sent to the papers were again full of the 'theory that human beings are descended from apes', as if that were the whole story.

'The unity of biochemistry'

Biochemistry is the science which studies what chemical reactions take place in living organisms, animals, plants and micro-organisms. There are now some millions of these. By far the majority of species had died out long before there were human beings. Much is known about the biochemistry of a few dozen of them. My estimate is that something is known of the biochemistry of not much more than a thousand species. What does that mean? A thousand kinds of biochemistry? Fortunately not, since in that case biochemistry would be a hopeless discipline. The same components and the same reactions are to be found in lions and snapdragons. There are certainly biochemical differences, but they are far less striking than the agreements. This concept was worked out by the Delft microbiologist A. J. Kluyver in 1926 in a publication entitled *Die Einheit in der Biochemie*, and is now internationally known as the unity of biochemistry.

Since the 1970s biochemistry has been in a position to establish the order of the elements of DNA (denoted with the letters A, C, G, and T) with great rapidity and precision. Similarly, it is possible to establish the order of the amino-acids in a protein molecule. A protein usually consists of several hundred amino-acids; twenty different amino-acids are used to form proteins, the same twenty for each form of life. DNA, the vehicle of hereditary characteristics, contains the information for the amino-acid sequence of each protein in code-form, the genetic code. DNA consists of a double helix of two complementary strands wound around each other: they are complementary because there is a base A opposite each base T and a base G opposite each base C. The DNA of a bacterium is a double helix of around 4 million base pairs in which the genes are closely packed together. A gene is a bit of DNA which contains the information for a protein. Each of the cells in the human body contains a thousand times as much DNA as a bacterium. It is not that we are a thousand times as complicated as a bacterium: far from it. But our genes are wider apart and are interrupted by bits of DNA which do not code for an amino-acid sequence. Around 90% of our DNA has little or no clear function. Human beings and many other animals and plants are effective means of spreading DNA around themselves on this planet – yet another completely different perspective from which one can look at evolution.

Computer genealogies

The previous section on the unity of biochemistry is a necessary interlude which makes it possible finally to demonstrate the overwhelming number of indications of the correctness of the theory of evolution. From a comparison of the anatomy of plants and animals, and from palaeontology (the theory of fossils), a grouping (taxonomy) of the plant and animal kingdom is inferred which claims to give as good an account as possible of the relationship of species.

One can get similar information from the basic sequence of related genes in number of species. The same is true if a comparison is made of the sequence of amino-acids of corresponding proteins in different species; the amino-acid sequences are always a translation of related genes. If rabbit, hare, mouse and rat have a particular protein fragment in a particular position in a corresponding protein with the composition *val-asa-ser-glu-glu* (three-letter abbreviations of amino acids), and dog, cat and bear have *val-ala-ser-asp-glu* in that fragment, this indicates that dog, cat and bear had a common ancestor which is related to, but not an ancestor of, rabbit, hare, mouse and rat.

Of course such a mutation (*glo/asp*) is far too little to draw any conclusion from. However, one hundred mutations in one protein are enough to make a whole genealogy of organisms with a computer programme. And of course the same is true of DNA fragments.

By now long pieces of DNA have been 'sequenced', in total 800 million base pairs; many from human beings, but also many from all kinds of other organisms. The amino-acid sequence of tens of thousands of proteins has been established, and of many proteins in dozens of organisms. So numerous genealogies have been made with computer programmes. Details of difference apart, these genealogies match the palaeontological and anatomical genealogy admirably. Moreover they supplement it, where strong anatomical likeness of some species gives no information about their mutual relationship. We can go even further: knowing from palaeontology that rodents began to form a separate group within mammals around forty million years ago, we can investigate how quickly a particular protein develops: for example, one in a hundred amino-acids in five million years. This knowledge can be used to estimate how long ago other particular splits took place when there is no palaeontological evidence. One can make the estimate more accurate by taking into account the speed of the mutation of different proteins or DNA fragments.

Creationists usually argue that the homology between genes and proteins of different sorts can also be explained by assuming that God intelligently made use of the same motives in creation. If that were true, it would mean that God did this in such an ingenious way that whatever protein or DNA fragment one analyses, it would always seem that the species derived from each other in one and the same way, in just the same way as they also seem to derive from one another on the basis of their anatomy and palaeontology. Is it perhaps God's purpose for us to believe in evolution?

Evolution in the school-leaving examination

I remarked earlier that fundamentalists and natural scientists comfortably ignore one another's existence. Interested as we biologists are in the history of our discipline, of course we know how Darwin's theory divided people in the nineteenth century. But now, we thought, the concept of evolution has become commonplace. People have become familiar with the mutual relationship between species, with the time-scale of our earth and with fossils. In the bookshops there are books about animal psychology from which it is evident that the difference between human beings and animals is gradual rather than absolute. Opposition to the theory of evolution is a rear-guard action, we thought, which takes place in conservative areas in the Netherlands and in some American states, like Alabama. Wasn't Alabama also the state in which the authorities wanted to fix the figure π at 3.14 precisely, so that young people didn't need to learn irrational numbers? No wonder that biologists thought that they could ignore the fight against the theory of evolution.

And what happened suddenly in Holland, our enlightened country which we ourselves thought to be so sober? An old-fashioned dispute about Darwin arose in the schools. It's too embarrassing for words. It is only fortunate that news of events in the Netherlands has such difficulty in getting known abroad. We are really ashamed to tell our colleagues.

The origin of life

Even before Darwin, the creation story was not maintained in a completely consistent way. Earlier, people were generally convinced that smaller animals, like insects, the procreation of which often escaped perception, came into being spontaneously. I even once found in an eighteenth-century book a recipe for making mice: one puts a box of wheat in an attic . . . Only around 1860 did Louis Pasteur demonstrate that the growth of micro-organisms in a medium could not be attributed to spontaneous generation. 'Pasteurize' became a term in food technology, but the discovery also had a great influence on our collective biological insight. After all, once, more than three billion years ago, life appeared on earth. What we know, or think we know about that, has implications, but this is not part of the theory of evolution. I shall end this article with a brief description of how according to the present state of science we imagine the appearance of life on earth.

Four billion years ago the atmosphere had a different composition from now. In addition to the vapour, nitrogen and carbon gas that we know, presumably it also contained carbon monoxide, ammonia, methane and even prussic acid, but no oxygen. In 1953 Miller and Urey demonstrated in laboratory experiments that electronic discharges (imitating storms) and ultraviolet light (which before there was oxygen in the atmosphere was not yet held back with an ozone layer) in such a mixture of gas led to the formation of amino-acids, sugars and other substances which even now are still the chemical elements of life. Probably the lakes, pools and seas in this way became a breeding ground, so called Oparin's soup (named after a pioneer in this sphere, Alexander Oparin). By the condensation of these nutrients, probably after the absorption of minerals, DNA-like polymers must then have formed, presumably a substance related to ribonucleic acid (RNA), which here for the sake of convenience I shall call primal RNA.

Like present-day RNA, this primal RNA can act as an enzyme, in other words as a biological catalyst, in the way that we find above all in proteins (enzymes). It must be assumed that in these kinds of processes, over the course of millions of years primal RNA molecules also originated which were capable of replicating themselves. Now the survival of the fittest came into effect: the molecules which could do this best and most quickly began to dominate in the population. But with the increasing complexity of these polymers their vulnerability also increased. This led through further selection to primal RNA, which saw a chance to cover itself with a fatty membrane: the first primitive cells.

In the first hundreds of millions of years such primitive cells will have come into being and been lost again in many places on earth. Finally a strong type won the battle: a primal bacterium which had learned to make proteins as well as RNA, and which could turn its primal genes into the form of the chemically more stable DNA. This in its need for energy provided itself with nutriment from Oparin's soup and through a primitive metabolism turned this into lactic acid and ammonia. To make proteins, this primal bacterium developed a genetic code to translate a basic series in a nucleic acid into the amino-acid sequence of a protein. Since all plants, animals and micro-organisms today use the same basic code, we assume that we and everything else derive from this primal bacterium.

The blessings of an ecological crisis

The primal bacterium and many of the other bacteria derived from it spread steadily until the Oparin's soup was used up. With that, growth came to a standstill, but not evolution. Bacteria arrived which had the capacity to use the energy from sunlight to make nutriment from simpler chemical combinations (photosynthesis); in the long run they even made hydrogen out of water, thus giving birth to an inexhaustible source of energy. This is also what our present-day plants do, and what our whole energy management is based on: we eat plants or animals, which live on plant-like food. These developments took place very early in evolution, for traces of the products of photosynthesis have been found already in geological formations from 3.8 billion years ago.

Photosynthesis also has a disadvantage. The photosynthetic dissolution of water also releases oxygen, a reactive gas which was deadly for life on earth at that time, at least in high concentrations. And it was not long before there were high concentrations: there is much argument over precisely how long. Estimates of the oxygen content in the atmosphere a billion years ago vary from one to ten per cent. Even if we accept the low estimate, this was a direct threat to all the life at the time: an ecological crisis compared with which all the environmental problems caused by human beings are negligible. It was at that time, between 700 million and 1 billion years ago, that nature/evolution/the Creator made the greatest invention since the origin of life: breathing. Bacteria arose which made a virtue of necessity: they began to use oxygen for a more complete transformation of nutrients. Lactic acid was further broken down into carbon gas and water. In this way a molecule of sugar provided eighteen times as much energy as before. At the same time proteins and vitamins were developed in order to protect the precious DNA as well as possible from oxygen.

Without this breakthrough there would never have been multicellular organisms, plants and animals. They would have needed so much food, eighteen times more than we do, that the consumption and digestion of it – also processes requiring energy – would have come up against insoluble logistical problems. Through breathing we could become complicated animals with muscles, sense organs and brains.

A true explosion of new forms of life took place from these first breathers. The earth changed from an empty service into the luxurious paradise in which the first human beings lived a few million years ago, breathing air with say 21% oxygen. But we have paid a price for our multicellular nature and the use of the dangerous oxygen: we are no longer potentially immortal, like our constantly dividing unicellular ancestors. The protection of our DNA against oxygen is incomplete. The day will come when we have acquired so much wear and tear on the hundreds of billions of cells in our body that we get an incurable cancer, a heart attack or a brain haemorrhage, or we just die of the general weakness that we call old age.

Translated by John Bowden

The Theory of Evolution as a Megatheory of Western Thought

HERMANN HÄRING

Traditional metaphysics begins from a proud basic thesis: there is one immutable divine truth and this is independent of coming into being and passing away, life and death. In principle the human spirit can recognize this truth. Until well into modern times Western culture has understood life against this background. Life is formed and given directly by God. The manifold species of plants and animals exist in accordance with the divine plan. Therefore they have an existence which transcends the time and history of individual living beings.[1] For the human person, that is true to a tremendous degree, for each human soul is directly created by God. It is spirit, immortal and ultimately not subject to the laws of biological life.[2] On the contrary, through the soul every human being is ordained for a higher, spiritual goal. All that we know about biological life could in the end only serve as a heuristic metaphor for this real life, as an illustration of its primal idea. For centuries this was the primal conviction, the frame of reference of all further thought and culture.

The theory of evolution brought about a radical break with this. As the article by Bloemers shows, it brings physics and cosmology, biology and biochemistry, anthropology and epistemology into an overall connection. It, and not philosophical counter-theories, has finally led to the end of metaphysics and an anthropology of the spirit. Formerly the spirit formed the great framework of reality. Now the course of development of the cosmos as life holds the universe together from its origins to its end. This is an earthly material life which develops from itself, supports itself and – perhaps in accordance with an unknown plan – keeps unfolding. Life (now used in the singular) becomes the decisive, almost miraculous, basic dynamic of our reality which is always at work. This theory of evolution in the comprehensive sense of the world has quasi-mythical, almost religious features. In this article, which is simply meant to comment on the article which precedes it, I have called the theory of evolution the megatheory of Western culture. What is meant by that?

I. The world-view of the contemporary: objective, correct, authentic

Many years ago, Habermas pointed out that the truth of a statement extends to many dimensions.[3] The core of a truth certainly rests in what – simply and without any further considerations or qualifications – we call 'ontologically' or 'objectively' true, 'in accordance with reality'. Such statements say 'what is the case'. There are statements which so to speak explain themselves from what they denote. The content of their information corresponds to reality itself, as is presupposed by all correspondence theories.[4] Such truth can be tested objectively and handed on as information. Thus, for example, the statement that each child receives its life from its parents can be checked by reality and possibly refuted. The same goes for the assertion that all life developed from a first living being, a 'primal cell'.[5] We deal daily with this truth in information in which the subject-matter itself is presented. In the light of their ideal of truth, the natural sciences try to get close to the subject of their study. There is no doubt that those working on the theory of evolution attempt with their instruments, as scientifically as possible, to track down the truth understood in this way. It has to be possible to justify the theory of evolution, otherwise it must disappear from the text books.

But from Darwin to the present day both the triumphal progress of the theory of evolution and the many controversies over it point to a second dimension of truth. This triumphal process took place not only in science but also in Western societies.[6] So at the same time there is the question how a group, a society or a culture relates to certain statements. Truth aims to be effective. It develops a social force or social restrictions; it is regarded as 'right' or 'wrong' and becomes the element which binds people in a group, a friendly or a hostile element. Thus to objective truth is added a social 'rightness' which at the same time both interprets reality and society and enables communication about them; now, for example, social events can be understood as a 'struggle for survival'. This social dimension of a statement comes close to the social system which brings about community, and joins together common convictions and values. One thinks of the crescent and the cross, the tricolour, the confession of human dignity or the doctrine of justification in the Lutheran tradition. In past decades the theory of evolution has had such an effect. It has become the symbol and sign of a type of thought which affirms life, which inserts human beings into the stream of all life and puts all life into the context of the all-embracing cosmic reality.

It is presumably these all-embracing points of reference which have made the theory of evolution a component of the Western view of the world and of life which is accepted everywhere, Now a scientific theory need not be ashamed of guiding comprehensive interpretations, bonding and mobilizing social forces. But such cultural and social backing makes science prone to go beyond its bounds, to the point of claiming to be a substitute for philosophy and religion. I shall return to that later.

Nevertheless, before it becomes a statement, every insight begins with individual discoveries. Truth begins with the assertion of individuals: the I is the indispensable presupposition of every (new) statement. The analysis of a statement is completely satisfactory only when the person who makes it is included: 'I say or assert, doubt, hope or conjecture that something is the case and not otherwise.' And all those who accept this statement have to ask themselves the question, 'What do I personally think of it?' Therefore every statement is either honest or lying, an expression of a conviction to the point of making an unconditional claim or indifferent repetition, a warning or a promise. Assertions always contain such an element of personal commitment. I put myself in the middle of the context asserted, and to this degree all language – more or less – means action.[7] The purely descriptive, absolutely objective reproduction of states of affairs is always a dangerous limit case, to the point of meaningless chatter. To say that the theory of evolution makes an intense demand on people needs no further justification here. Those who acknowledge it put themselves in a context of biological life. The old and banal question whether human beings are descended from apes therefore still always gives the same clear signal. The theory of evolution affects the whole of humanity in its self-understanding. Above all it, affects a culture which has attached the utmost significance to reality – something that differentiates us qualitatively from the animal. Those who accept the theory of evolution firmly as a statement about themselves are immediately asked about the authenticity of their own convictions.

Accord with reality, social acceptance and authenticity, these three dimensions are therefore strongly and equally marked in the theory of evolution. Three agents are involved – the subject, the community and the individual concerned – and they come together here. The claim to scientific objectivity, the bond through social plausibility and the challenge to the individual self-understanding to a large degree supplement and reinforce one another. That is certainly a first reason why the theory of evolution is so taken for granted, so omnipresent and so interesting in Western culture.

Those who engage in it experience science at first hand, take their place among their contemporaries, and learn a great deal, perhaps even the decisive things, about themselves. Those who do not engage in this comprehensive and topical world-view are fools.

II. An expansive interpretation of the world: life, cosmos and mind

However, the theory of evolution was not and is not a new achievement; the idea was already there before Darwin. The long prehistory can be read in any lexicon. To begin with, the question of descent, i.e. our origin, and not the problem of life stands at the centre. The first theories of descent already appear in the Enlightenment (1707–1778). Even C. Linné (1707–1778), the scholar well known for his arguments for the constancy of the species, who arranged them in a model system of genera, families, orders and classes, toyed with the notion that to begin with many species were a single species. Further theorists (including Darwin's grandfather) followed and were to continue to follow. Charles Darwin could discuss his theories for years with colleagues who thought similarly and presented their views in many writings. His classic work *On the Origin of Species* (1859) became established for two reasons. On a visit to the Galapagos Islands he was able to produce an impressive and overwhelmingly large amount of material, and in accordance with a basic scientific principle he interpreted genealogies not teleologically but causally. For him the principle of selection became decisive.

There is no doubt that the theory of the descent and 'development' of all living beings from a single origin can be accepted today as scientifically assured; some articles in this issue also attest this. No one can escape the theory as such. In the present state of the discussion, other theories, like creationism, which seems almost absurd, are dependent on the construction of complicated auxiliary theories; nor are there any counter-theories with equally good infrastructures. But the reason for the success of this theory is not only its acceptance by society but its capacity to absorb further theories or to adopt them as expansions of its own scheme.

Some references may illuminate this. Darwin only hesitantly incorporated human beings into the event of evolution. However, the consistency of the theory proved stronger. A century later (after a certainly laborious course involving much hostility), on the whole to include human beings in the theory of evolution is no longer felt to be an insult to humankind. Early theoreticians of evolution, however, believed that they could use it to destroy the Christian structure of faith. But, at the latest, since Teilhard de Chardin and Karl Rahner the decisive resistance has been removed, especially as the question of 'monogenism' has been solved; humankind need not necessarily be descended from a single human couple.[8] In addition there was the question of the beginning of life in the strict sense, on which Darwin had not yet expressed himself, but about which clear theories would develop in the twentieth century. Meanwhile the experiment with Oparin soup described in the first article has established itself in the collective consciousness. Finally biochemistry, as has also been explained, has led to clear, very differentiated but also highly fascinating notions about the highly complex chemistry of the beginning of life. Since the 1950s, when scientists began to analyse DNA more closely, the theory of descent has not needed to be corrected. On the contrary, in the mind of the public it has now finally deepened into the theory of evolution.

At the same time an important supplement to the theory of evolution has developed. This comprises models of the development of the cosmos, to the construction of which E. Hubble (1929) made a decisive contribution. In his view the cosmos had a dynamic of constant expansion, and this led to the – not uncontroversial – notion of a Big Bang (fifteen to twenty billion years ago), a pulsating or ultimately dispersing universe. Within this comprehensive 'history' of the cosmos the tremendous events of the origination of spiral nebulae and galaxies, of exploding stars which collapse in on themselves, or suns and planetary systems, is played out. Finally, these events include – at a chance point in endless space and at a closely defined point within gigantic periods of time – the earth. The history of life and the world are thus once again set in such a framework that the classical theory of evolution is taken up into a far more comprehensive event of evolution.[9] We interpret our life here and now and still hear the background noises of the beginnings. The theory of evolution could not have expanded outwards more dramatically, catching the human imagination.

But the integrative force of the theory of evolution is not yet exhausted by this. At present the greatest fascination is doubtless exercised by biogenetics. As we already saw, this is still caught up in an explosive development. It began with the discovery of DNA, with the deciphering of the structure of the cell and access to what could be called the mystery of life, at any rate the mystery of reduplication and heredity. New life always comes into being through the unpredictable combination of two lines of inheritance; the genetic inheritance reconstitutes itself each time. We are on the track of the framework of possible heredity and mutation, and have even calculated spans of time for particular leaps in mutation. Many scientists see in this development the decisive concentration and confirmation of the theory of evolution. What so far had been supported 'only' phenomenologically and – very weakly – on the basis of archaeological discoveries is now given an irrefutable, as it were inner, confirmation which can be interpreted by mathematics. Here processes in life which show as it were the origin of the great beginning in every life that begins anew are evident from within. What happens here is – finally – an irrefutable event which constantly repeats itself and can be analysed empirically.[10]

It is as if the theory of evolution is finally reaching the area of demonstrable facticity. Here continuity and discontinuity can be attained, and the proximity or distance between species can virtually be calculated. Whereas the classical theory of descent with its arguments from phenomenology and archaeology was always dependent on interpretations over a large area, had to seek ever new links and repeatedly change the geographical information, here firm ground has seemed to emerge. Here evolution has finally developed into an assured theory. However, amazingly, it remains the fact that after 150 years the old theory has not been displaced, but now at last has been brilliantly confirmed by the inner messages of cell structure and double helix. The theory of evolution has proved itself to be the leading theme of biogenetics; and it is to be fused with biogenetics into a comprehensive biotheory.

Here research into the brain is beginning to storm the last domain of the formation of genetic theory.[11] If we human beings are indebted to the great course of life, to its constantly higher development, then – for the theory to be consistent – consciousness and mind must also be explicable from the ever-higher development of material structures, and ultimately thus, as we shall see further below, as material phenomena. Now these theories about consciousness do not yet seem have matured on the basis of the theory of evolution. By that, I mean that work is still done with crude antitheses, with simplified models and with the solemnity of a final discovery, from which the smoke must clear by means of the discovery of qualifications. Sometimes it is again, and too simplistically, proclaimed that while human beings are descended from apes, the mind is descended from the electron. I am not saying explicitly that such theories are dead ends, for mature models have yet to be developed. But with this qualification we can foresee the day on which here too the model of evolution will prove its force. We will then not be humbling the spirit but finally giving matter and energy their due dignity. Perhaps only then will the true significance of Teilhard's Hymn to the Universe be recognized.

III. From world-view to ideology

However, current discussions about mind and consciousness show that with the epoch-making success and constant expansion of the theory of evolution more is at stake than the success of a scientific hypothesis. What is at stake is the still ongoing revolution in the understanding of the world, society and human beings which began in the nineteenth century and still is not finished. Here the dimensions of social acceptance and individual authenticity described above must not be left out of account. The theory of evolution has long since begun to reinterpret the world, society and the individual. Moreover it exercises an almost religious fascination on people.[12] It has the power of a world-view and is danger of being misused as an ideology. By world-view I mean the force I have mentioned with which it interprets the world, society and the individual, comprehensively and quasi-rationally, but at the same time graphically and deeply, as was once the case with Plato, the Stoa or the Thomistic system.

That is evident from the fact that it answers, or seems to answer, fundamentally anthropological and therefore highly significant questions. Who began the world and how is cosmic reality ultimately to be understood? What is the difference between 'dead' and 'living' matter, like matter and mind? Can't we explain the functions of the brain in terms of its material infrastructure? What is the difference between human beings and animals, and how are we to think of human dignity on the presuppositions of evolution? Here fundamentally philosophical questions are raised and posed in model contexts, but never directly answered. Many natural scientists are aware of this: the absolute beginning of the cosmos is no more explained than the actual transition to life. We know just as little about the actual origin (the 'fulguration', as Lorenz calls it) of the mind. But restraint is not always the strength of natural science. Scientists are fond of giving reductionist answers: life is then 'none other than' matter with a higher organization; spirit 'none other than' self-guidance mechanisms developed to perfection; human beings 'none other than' highly disciplined animals. 'None other than?' The miracle consists precisely in the fact that matter begins to live; that systems of digital guidance develop and experience a proximity to themselves; that higher animals can suddenly know, feel and love. In reality the natural scientists do not give any answers, but they do describe in a new way the mystery of the beginning of life and what we call the soul.

Questions of social significance follow and never come to rest. In view of what happens in nature, precisely what is the meaning of Darwin's principle of selection, the survival of the fittest? What is the significance of the dispute over the absence or effectiveness of a teleological principle and what is a successful causal effect? What are we to think of the selfish gene (Dawkins), and how far are the ethical approaches of socio-biology (Wilson) convincing? The significance of these elements of theory is constantly discussed, but the ethical conclusions are by no means convincing. Nevertheless, the suggestive power of the great formulae is constantly being established. They are used to legitimate social conditions: the selfishness of individuals, the questionable nature of capitalism, the power of vital drives. At this point, world-view becomes ideology, i.e. the legitimation of what benefits us. Therefore at this point, at the same time questions of religious significance emerge. Does the theory of evolution perhaps contradict a religious, especially a monotheistic, interpretation of the world? Of course theology has devised answers which resolve this contradiction and show it up to be false. Nevertheless, it is striking how for many people the notion of God's action is quite incompatible with the notion of the self-organization of the cosmos, life or mind.[13] The last word has yet to be spoken on the differences between this scientifically empirical language and a religious one.

I shall break off the catalogue of questions here. They cannot be discussed at length in this context. But these questions can show one thing: in the controversy over the theory of evolution, for theology and faith nothing and at the same time everything is at stake.[14] Nothing decisive is at stake, since here the sciences with their instruments (the methods of archaeology and astrology, biogenetics and computer simulation, chemistry and nuclear physics) are simply explaining our reality (the cosmos, life and human beings) in the light of its origin. Theology and faith must be grateful for that, since every detail that we discover in reality helps us to understand the world and ourselves better. It helps us to encounter the mystery of the world, to experience God. Certainly, Dawkins is naïve to claim that the biblical creation story is extremely boring by comparison with a textbook on biogenetics. But the wealth of what we have by now come to know about organic and human life has become enormous. The experience of God who is life has thus expanded; for the view of this world always has something to do with the view of God. And we must not forget that Christians and other believers are children of this age. We too contribute these new models, possibilities and experiences. Seen in a proper light, faith is therefore neither endangered nor replaced.

At the same time something decisive is at stake. The theory of evolution, the megatheory of Western culture, incessantly offers surpluses of models of explanation, interpretation and action. It surprises us with constantly new insights. It gives the impression that it could explain the origin of the world, the 'leap' from nothingness to being, as if it were replacing the defective explanation or an obsolete and prescientific religion. Our societies also perceive the theory of evolution as an arsenal for the foundation of a new, predominantly capitalist, ethic. This is to overlook that conversely the theorists of evolution flee into social metaphors: into struggle, competition and a merciless 'Those who do not establish themselves go under!' In a naïve ploy, the mind is reduced to the interaction of a computer game. And just as forty years ago the elite were still terrified with human beings as 'naked apes', so today they are shocked with the robot as an image, confronted with the horror of a race which clones itself.

IV. What is to be done?

So the question is: how can we take the theory of evolution seriously as a scientific theory and at the same time unmask its ideological violations of frontiers? Is there a way between fundamentalist opposition and uncritical acceptance? The answer to this question must begin with a self-critical observation. It is one of the tragedies of Western history that for centuries the churches and theology have forced the natural sciences into an unnecessary opposition. Despite papal offers of reconciliation,[15] the effects of this have yet to be overcome. So it is not surprising that many scientists still do what the churches have for long enough accused them of doing (and what the creationists are again doing): they understand God a human super-father who is enthroned above the worlds and sometimes intervenes. Therefore they read biblical texts as accounts in the style of physics, religious statements as ontological information. They understand the biblical creation story as a naïve attempt at explanation and accounts of miracles as fables remote from the world. Clarity needs to be achieved here. The first problem is not what the theory of evolution has to say to believers. We should first of all clarify what religious experience and biblical tradition can say about world and life. They have no knowledge to communicate, but they do help us to discover traces of the divinely inexpressible.

Western culture first of all has the task of gaining a new and elementary access to religious experiences. The image of God in the monotheistic religions is tremendously complex.[16] Thus for example we can develop rationally convincing models for God's action which are acceptable to faith and the natural sciences. At the same time it needs to be shown that we will never exhaust the depths of religious experience. From a theological perspective the word of God, the action of God or God's presence are metaphors which go with talk of God's silence, absence or superiority. However vividly we can reconstruct the beginning of creation, the beginning and the development of life, we do not touch on the elementary experience of the miracle represented by creation, life and its evolution. Conversely, an unquenchable curiosity is part of religious experience, because the theory of evolution with its many facets also brings us nearer to the mystery of God. God is life. But God is also spirit: therefore our elementary religious curiosity will also be tremendously interested in future research into consciousness. Finally, the notion of evolution touches the core of elementary religious experience: we are taken up into the great lines of cosmic development and in particular we stand in a broad stream of the exchange of life, of physical receiving and giving, and the relationships from which in the end no living being is left out. Anyone who gains a new and elementary access to religious experiences will experience knowledge about life and evolution as an enrichment.

At the same time, grappling with the theory of evolution in all its branches can compel us to understand the message of the Bible anew. Some examples of this are given in this issue. In general it will prove that of course the model of creation and life given there has now been superseded, but that was not the aim of the texts. If the Bible sees, say, creation as the struggle of a life-enhancing order with deadly chaos, the topical message of such thought is clear. If at the same time the Bible puts the goodness of creation above all other statements about the world and history, then today once again the challenge of such an assertion can be felt. And to anyone who understands the contradictory multiplicity of biblical statements – about God's presence and distance, his action and his absence, about the goodness and cruelty of reality, about the struggle of the stronger and the power of weakness – will soon become clear that the Bible as a whole leads us, too, to grapple with this reality. According to the biblical ideal religion is manifestly no textbook on the state of God, human beings and the world but an occasion to grapple with weakness and violence, with love and hatred, with human physicality and individual dignity. It is not a matter of answers of a didactic kind but of our readiness to accept this world and our fellow human beings.

The biblical tradition sees human beings and the world as an event rooted in matter, as a physical event. At the same time its interest is not in teaching about the cosmos and life. Its interest is in our learning to regulate our human relationships in the face of God, to accept others, like ourselves, as the image of God. This perspective makes it clear how Christians can affirm and follow critically the tremendously fruitful model of evolution.

Translated by John Bowden

Notes

1. The 1993 *Catechism of the Catholic Church* still speaks in a relatively undifferentiated way of an 'ordered and good world' (no. 299). Moreover: 'Each of the various creatures, willed in its own being, reflects in its own way a ray of God's infinite wisdom and goodness' (no. 339). Thus an awareness of evolution is carefully bracketted out. The same is true of the article on 'Life' in the latest edition of the *Lexikon für Theologie und Kirche*, 1997, 714–16.
2. This statement too is repeated with relatively little qualification by the *Catechism of the Catholic Church* (no. 366). 'The Church teaches that every spiritual soul is created immediately by God').
3. J. Habermas, *Theory of Communicative Action* I, Oxford 1985.
4. Correspondence theories explain the truth, as already did Thomas Aquinas, as a correspondence between the thing and the intellect. Thus they presuppose that reality can be known and described. Cf. L. B. Puntel, *Wahrheitstheorien in der neueren Philosophie*, Darmstadt 1983, 26–40.
5. I shall not go here into the differentiated theories of a hypothetical primal organism, or into the prior stages of the pre-, proto- and eobions (W. K. Purves et al., *Life: The Science of Biology*, Sunderland, Mass [4]1995).
6. This triumphant progress is usually discussed under terms like 'Darwinism' or 'Neo-Darwinism' (E. Mayr, *One Long Argument*, London 1993).
7. The brief book by J. L. Austin, *How to Do Things with Words*, Oxford [3]1980, is still the pioneer in this insight.
8. P. Overhage and K. Rahner, *Das Problem der Hominisation*, Freiburg 1961; P. A. Mellars and C. B. Stringer, *The Human Revolution*, Edinburgh 1989.
9. S. W. Hawking, *A Brief History of Time. From Big Bang to Black Holes*, London and New York 1988; J. M. Zyzinski, 'Metaphysics and Epistemology in Stephen Hawking's Theory of the Creation of the Universe', in *Zygon. Journal of Religion and Science* 31, 1996, 269–89.
10. The success of R. Dawkins, *The Blind Watchmaker*, Harlow 1986; id., *The Selfish Gene*, Oxford 1989; id., *River Out of Eden*, New York 1995, and other books is significant for fascination with these developments.
11. D. C. Dennett, *Darwin's Dangerous Idea*, New York 1995; D. Linke, *Das Gehirn*, Munich 1999; E. A. Wilson, *Neural Geographics*, New York and London 1998.

12. A. R. Peacocke, *God and the New Biology*, San Francisco 1986.
13. There is an extensive discussion of the problem – in connection with Whitehead – in P. M. F. Oomen, *Doet God ertoe? Een interpretatie van Whitehead als bijdrage aan een theologie van Gods handeln*, Kampen 1998.
14. P. Oomen, 'Theologie – exacte weetschappen: Een asymmetrische verouding', in R. van der Brandt and R. Plum (eds), *De theologie uitgedaagt. Spreken over God binnen het weetschapsbedrijf*, Zoetermeer 1999, 35–60; F. Watts, 'Are Science and Region in Conflict?', *Zygon* 32, 1997, 125–38.
15. *Osservatore Romano*, 24 October 1996.
16. J. Miles, *God. A Biography*, New York 1995.

II. The Significance of Evolutionary Theory in the Present

The Evolution of the Cosmos and of Life

GEORGES DE SCHRIJVER

In this article I would like to examine the challenges that current cosmological paradigms pose to theology today. In terms of physics, these paradigms try to answer the questions: How did it all start? What do we, as human beings, owe to the prolonged expansion of the universe and the formation of galaxies in it? Questions about the origin of the universe have always aroused the interest of theologians, but today the search for the 'point' where it all started has been severed from the question of God. For a long time now, scientists have espoused a methodological atheism, although this attitude does not prevent them from experiencing at times a sense of cosmic awe. However, recourse to the metaphysical first cause is not part of the dealings of astrophysics. We are far removed from the piety of Newton, who still saw in the order of nature the sovereign and operative might of the Pantokrator imposing his will on all created things.

I. Big Bang theory

Canon Georges le Maître, priest-mathematician at Louvain University, member of the Pontifical Academy of Astronomy, and one of the pioneers of the Big Bang theory, knew of this separation between science and faith, and attempted in vain to dissuade Pius XII from engaging in theological comments on the Big Bang. These might be understood, Le Maître feared, as putting a scientific theory in the service of faith. But does the imagination not suggest an association between the explosive eruption of an ocean of fire giving birth to the universe and the opening verses of Genesis: 'And God said, "Let there be light"'? For scientists, however, this event is not just an issue of piety. For them the Big Bang is the initial bursting forth of space-time and with it the release of a stupendous energy formative of the universe.

To grasp this scientific concern, a brief evocation of some early twentieth-century milestones in the research of astrophysics is in place. In 1915 Albert Einstein developed the general theory of relativity which states that space curves under the influence of gravitational fields. 'Einstein made the revolutionary suggestion that gravity is not a force like other forces, but is a consequence of the fact that space-time is "warped", by the distribution of mass and energy in it.'[1] One of the consequences of the theory is that the cosmos as a whole is caught up in a dynamics of becoming: the universe ought to be in a state of either expansion or contraction. But Einstein resented this idea. So he thought he had made a mistake in his calculations, and to avoid the abhorred instability of the universe, he introduced the cosmological constant. At this juncture, Le Maître took up Einstein's calculations and found out that there was no need to introduce such a constant. In 1927 he published a book in which he put forward the hypothesis that the cosmos must have expanded from a very dense primeval atom (today called singularity) which, 'in the beginning', exploded in a tremendous display of fireworks.[2] Some scientists suspected Le Maître of using this hypothesis to give credit to the biblical creation narrative. It would also take Einstein a long time eventually accept to Le Maître's intuition. He did so only after in 1929 Edwin Hubble provided empirical evidence of the expansion of the universe.

To situate Hubble, one must know something about the use he made of two important techniques that had been advanced in the first half of the nineteenth century: spectroscopy and the measurement of changing frequencies of waves. The first allows for identifying the physical properties of things using spectral analysis. E.g., by studying the spectrum of sunlight, one finds out that the sun contains helium, carbon, etc. Spectroscopy also allowed for identifying the chemistry of other stars in our galaxy, once appropriate telescopes became available. In fact, it turned out that all the stars in our Milky Way possess the same chemical make-up. There is thus no reason for us to boast that the place where we are living is something special. Second came the Doppler effect, named after its discoverer, who in his research on sound waves found that as the source emitting a sound (e.g. a car) approaches, it registers at a higher pitch (corresponding to a higher frequency of sound waves), and when it passes and goes away, it registers at a lower pitch (corresponding to a lower frequency).[3] The Doppler effect also obtains in the case of measuring the frequencies of light waves emitted by stars. A shift of a characteristic spectral pattern towards the blue end of the spectrum tells us that the source is coming nearer to us, whereas a move towards the red tells us that the source is receding from us (the so-called red-shift).

Hubble worked with one of the strongest telescopes of his time at the Mount Wilson Observatory in California. This allowed him to look into what till then were thought to be spiralling clouds of gas (nebulae), but turned out to be real galaxies outside our Milky Way. He was able to identify myriads of stars in them and get a picture of their chemistry. When he set out to calculate the distances of these galaxies from the earth, he found something most peculiar: in the spectra of stars in other galaxies 'there were the same characteristic sets of missing colours as for stars in our own galaxy, but they were all shifted by the same relative amount toward the red end of the spectrum'.[4] This meant that these stars and galactic clusters were receding. Hubble could even observe that the more distant a galaxy, the faster it is receding. If a galaxy located at a distance of fifty million light years from us is receding at a certain speed, a galaxy at twice that distance will recede at twice that speed.

II. In search of the chemistry of the early universe

This raises the question of the origin and the end of the universe.[5] Indeed, if the universe is still in a state of violent explosion, in which the great islands of stars known as galaxies are rushing apart at speeds approaching the speed of light, it must be possible to 'extrapolate this explosion backward in time and conclude that all the galaxies must have been much closer at the same time in the past – so close, in fact, that neither galaxies nor stars nor even atoms or atomic nuclei could have had a separate existence'.[6] This is the area close to the 'point' (the singularity) from where it all started some fifteen billion years ago, and which is generally called the early universe.

The initial singularity from which all that is burst forth is still largely unexplored. The reason is quite simple: In the first fractions of a second following the Big Bang, densities and temperatures were so great that conventional theories of matter break down. Einstein's theory of relativity is an excellent instrument for the study of macro-events (the recession of galaxies), but what is needed now is quantum physics and the study of radiation, as well as electrodynamics. The 'hot Big Bang theory', developed by George Gamov in 1948, and later refined with insights gained from nuclear reactions, finds its place here. The research, though, is not yet finished. Only a Grand Unified Theory (GUT) will be able to shed light on the primitive stage in which the four forces were still united and not separated as they are now. Research in this direction is already under way, e.g. in CERN (European Centre for Nuclear Research) near Geneva, where a gigantic particle accelerator provides experimental data for theory formation.

The reconstruction of the scenario reads as follows. At the Big Bang itself, the universe is thought to have had zero size, and to have been infinitely hot. Some fractions of a second later the universe would have contained mostly photons, i.e. quanta of radiating energy which have no mass and no electrical charge. These photons gave birth, through collisions, to particles and their corresponding anti-particles (these emerge in pairs, with opposite electrical charges), such as electrons (and their anti-particles 'positrons') and neutrinos (and their own anti-particles). When a particle and anti-particle meet, they annihilate each other in a flash of light to create energy – i.e. new photons which may dissolve again into matter-antimatter pairs etc. But 'as the universe expands, any matter or radiation in it gets cooler (when the universe doubles in size, its temperature falls by half)'.[7] So the behaviour in it may change. At a given moment a symmetry-break took place, in that more particles than anti-particles were created, so that for them annihilation stopped. If this 'accidental' symmetry-break had not occurred, the expanding universe would only have displayed a ballet of ever repeating flashes of light, with no viable matter in it – and thus with nothing that could lead to the emergence of life.[8] Moreover, if at a certain moment there would have been an overproduction of neutrinos, in certain circumstances this could have caused the universe to recollapse already at this early stage.[9]

So much is clear that one second after the Big Bang – with temperatures a thousand times the temperature at the centre of the sun – the stage was set for a 'laboratory' in which the building blocks of atoms (from quarks up to protons and neutrons) were formed, together with the forces that account for their organization and interaction. 'About one hundred seconds after the Big Bang, the temperature would have fallen to one thousand million degrees, the temperature inside the hottest stars.'[10] So protons and neutrons which had begun to lead a viable existence could no longer resist the strong nuclear force[11] and would have started to combine together to form the nuclei of atoms of heavy hydrogen (deuterium), made up of one proton and one neutron. These nuclei 'then would have combined with more protons and neutrons to make helium nuclei, which contain two protons and two neutrons, and also small amounts of a couple of heavier elements, lithium and beryllium'. In this way 'about a quarter of the protons and neutrons would have been converted into helium nuclei, along with a small amount of heavy hydrogen and other elements. The remaining neutrons would have decayed into protons, which are the nuclei of ordinary hydrogen atoms.'[12] The universe went on expanding and cooling, and nothing of more interest occurred for 300,000 years. At that time the temperature dropped a few thousand degrees to the point where nuclei and electrons can form atoms, the majority of them hydrogen and helium atoms. From these atoms, because of gravitation, clouds of gas were formed. And as these clouds got denser and denser, and hotter and hotter, galaxies made their appearance with stars in them – stars in which nuclear reactions convert hydrogen into more helium. When these stars happen to harbour planets, and when such a planet is close enough to the star to receive enough heat energy, and not too far from it to freeze, then the conditions are created for life to emerge.

The hot Big Bang theory is basically confirmed by the evidence we have of the microwave background which was detected in 1965 by Penzias and Wilson. With the help of a very sensitive microwave detector they picked up a very strange noise which was always the same , no matter in what direction the detector was pointed. By repeating this observation day and night, and in various seasons, they found out that the noise came from beyond our galaxy. Specialists in astrophysics made it clear to them that what they had captured were the traces of the fiery radiation emitted in the aftermath of the tremendously hot Big Bang explosion, a radiation which is reaching us now as microwaves.

III. The Anthropic Principle

The foregoing introduces us to the Anthropic Principle, which states that in some regions of the universe the physical conditions must have become such that they paved the way for beings like us, able to reconstruct their cosmic past. To these conditions belong what happened in the stars and in interstellar space. Indeed, for carbon-based life forms to appear, heavier elements than just helium and hydrogen are needed. Through further nuclear fusions the stars produce carbon, oxygen and iron which are indispensable for human life. When the first-generation stars exploded as supernovas, they scattered their life-generating elements into space, the explosion itself leading to the formation of still heavier elements such as zinc and iodine (iodine being essential to the healthy functioning of the thyroid gland). Our own sun 'is a second- or third-generation star, formed some five thousand million years ago out of a cloud of rotating gas containing the debris of earlier supernovas. Most of the gas in that cloud went to form the sun or got blown away, but a small amount of the heavier elements collected together to form the bodies that now orbit the sun as planets like the earth.'[13] One can say that we are made of the ashes of stars, that the iron in our blood has been formed in the stars.

John Polkinghorne reflects on these facts and points to the delicate balance presupposed in nuclear reactions: 'To make carbon in a star, three helium nuclei have to be made to stick together. This is tricky to achieve and only possible because a special effect (technically, a resonance) is present in just the right place. This delicate positioning depends upon the strong nuclear force that holds nuclei together. Change this force a little, and you lose the resonant effect.'[14] The same special effect is needed to produce oxygen (by making another helium nucleus stick to the carbon one). The list of this amazing fine-tuning can easily be extended. For stars to burn uniformly for a long period of time a delicate balance between gravity and electromagnetism is needed. If this balance is disturbed, 'the stars either become too cool to act as effective energy sources, or so hot that they burn away in a matter of a mere few million years'.[15] A further point of amazement is that both the age and the size of the universe concur in the process. Only a cosmos at least as big as ours – with its trillions upon trillions of stars – 'could endure for the fifteen billion years necessary for evolving carbon-based life. You need ten billion years for the first-generation stars to make the carbon, then about five billion years for evolution to yield beings of our sort of complexity.'[16]

This brings us again to the early universe. Stephen Hawking writes: 'If the rate of expansion one second after the Big Bang had been smaller by even one part in a hundred thousand million million, the universe would have recollapsed before it ever reached it present size. On the other hand, if it had been greater by a part in a million, the universe would have expanded too rapidly for stars and planets to form.'[17] Due to the fine-tuning of the expansion, our universe is largely smooth and regular. Had this not been the case, then catastrophic turbulences might have occurred already in the crucial initial phases of its existence. On the other hand the law of smoothness and regularity has proven to be flexible. Just think of the symmetry-break between matter and antimatter which led to the separation of radiation and matter. And also of the fact – discovered by the NASA satellite Cobe (Cosmic Background Explorer), launched in November 1989 – that the microwave background displays ripples, which means that 300,000 years after the Big Bang some regions had begun to amass more atoms than others. This fluctuation, too, seems to have been 'planned', for without this uneven amassment the universe would not have been able to be filled with scattered galaxies and stars.

It is at this juncture that the Anthropic Principle matters. The principle was launched by B. Carter. It states that the fundamental constants of nature must be such that 'what we expect to observe must be restricted to the conditions necessary for our presence as observers . . . The universe must be such as to admit the creation of observers within it at some stage.'[18] In other words, we live in a very special universe, one in which life and intelligence are possible. So, we look for the steps in the evolution of the universe that allow for the fact of our existence. This does not necessarily reflect an anthropocentric perspective. It rather underlines the need for us to realize that we belong to a cosmos that has the power to 'generate' us. There exists a deep connection between how matter came to be processed in the cosmos and our carbon-based, intelligent life.

IV. Belief in God: A disputed question

The Anthropic Principle, at first glance, seems a resuscitation of the design argument which for many centuries has been used to prove the existence of God.[19] But this is not exactly the case. It rather ushers in a divide between theistic and non-theistic scientists – between believers in God and believers in the forces of nature.

When theistic believers set out to reflect, from their biblical background, on the various fine-tunings that are presupposed to produce carbon-based intelligent life forms like ours, they will have no difficulty at all in associating these balanced choices with the God almighty 'who in the beginning created heaven and earth'. For them the fine-tunings, in the primal beginning and in the subsequent stages of development of the universe, all testify to the power and the intelligence of a Creator who apparently was eager to be accompanied by creatures that (to certain degrees) are made 'in his image'. With the help of science these believers begin to see many reasons for praising the patience and the generosity of the creator. Feelings of awe and admiration well up in them when they realize to what extent their life-opportunities have also been shaped through the mediation of so many evolutionary cosmic formations. When they know a bit about ancient 'Christianized' cosmologies, in which the angels in the starry sky played a decisive role in guaranteeing the continuation of life on earth (the angels provided energy to the spheres on which the planets orbited), they will even begin to look at the stars with feelings of awe, realizing that in these stars the chemical elements of their human bodies have been produced. They will perhaps understand better now what it means that cosmic potencies are used by the Creator/Sustainer to act as second causes in the process of creation.

Those belonging to the other camp, however, have their own reasons for refusing to associate the Anthropic Principle with a personal God. For them theories of multiple-universes constitute an alternative to theism. What these theories have in common is an intent to honour the role of chance, even with respect to fine-tuned initial conditions. Many scenarios are available.[20] A first one focusses on the 'successive cycles' an oscillating universe may go through. When a universe eventually melts down (Big Crunch) the conditions are prepared for a new Big Bang – and so on. Given quantum uncertainties, successive universes could be born with slightly varying constants. It is only by chance that a universe comes into being with carbon-based life in it. A second scenario admits of only one Big Bang, which, however, leads to the branching off of 'multiple isolated domains'. This scenario is a variant of the 'inflationary theory' which states that in the first fraction of a second the universe expanded with an exponential speed higher than the speed of light, thus 'inflating' the quasi-zero state of the universe into the kind of universe observed today. From this the Russian astrophysicist Andrei Linde deduced that inflating bubbles like this could have happened in various places. The early universe might have branched out into multiple bubbles which from the outside look extremely small, but which harbour within them cosmic regions as big as our universe. What sort of life might have been evolved in these bubbles cannot be verified, for each bubble is an isolated domain with its own variety of physical constants.

A third scenario is the 'many-worlds quantum theory', which reflects on the changes brought about in the quantum behaviour by the observer. Every time a quantum is being observed it splits, giving rise to two different worlds. This branching off can go on indefinitely. All the more reason then for attributing to chance which sort of life, if any, might emerge in so many regions of space-time. Multiple-universes are inevitable. The fourth scenario delves into the vacuum before the Big Bang, where quantum fluctuations emerge. Quantum theory permits very brief violations of the law of conservation of energy. In such a vacuum short-lived pairs of virtual particles can be born – from 'nothing', since they borrow energy from other short-lived pairs of virtual particles, then to service back their debt by disappearing through mutual annihilation. Now these exchanges of energy can lead to fluctuations which, if they are strong enough, can trigger a Big Bang not just once but on several occasions.

These scenarios are largely speculative, but can be calculated mathematically. They also seem convincing to philosophers who are interested in probability calculus – an enterprise which is going to trivialize the Anthropic Principle in so far as it may awaken people to cosmic awe. Indeed, probability calculus takes it for granted that in spite of so many misses a score of good luck must inevitably arrive. In a lottery there is always a winner; but it need not necessarily be you. Pondering on this state of affairs, John Leslie writes: 'Those living beings (who have made it), while having cause to thank their luck, could seem to have little ground for astonishment.'[21] This statement reveals a certain respect for the cosmic life forces, but also an undercurrent of resignation. For Leslie it is sufficient that things just happen as they are. For him the matter-of-factness of occurrences is enough to live by. At this juncture, however, one sees a parting of the ways taking place by those who believe in a personal God. Theologians like Polkinghorne, Barbour and Segundo – who are all cognizant of the newest developments in astrophysics – have also come to recognize the chance factor. But for them 'chance' is not just fatality. It is the breeding forth of new possibilities without which life would not be creative. At any rate this is the lesson they draw for their personal existence from the adventure of cosmic processes.[22] These processes keep alive a sense of wonder and awe which makes these theologians confess that the God who 'makes all things new' (Rev. 21.5) is deeply involved in his creation.

Notes

1. S. Hawking, *A Brief History of Time*, New York and London 1989, 32.
2. In 1922 the Russian mathematician, Alexander Friedmann, had already succeeded in solving Einstein's gravitational equations under the assumption of an expanding universe and an initial singularity. Le Maître worked independently of him.
3. Hawking, *Brief History* (n.1), 41.
4. Ibid., 40.
5. As far as the end is concerned, there are three scenarios which all tell that the universe is still in expansion. But at a critical moment a change will set in: (a) The model of the closed universe predicts that the impressive expansion will be followed by an equally impressive contraction. (b) The second model, that of

the open universe, conceives the universe as expanding so rapidly that the gravitational attraction can never stop it, though it does slow it down a bit. (c) The third model is that of Einstein–de Sitter: here, the universe is expanding just fast enough to avoid re-collapse.

6. S. Weinberg, *The First Three Minutes: A Modem View of the Origin of the Universe,* London 1986, 20.
7. Hawking, *Brief History* (n.1), 122.
8. Anti-matter, which has not been observed to exist in nature, would be a kind of matter made up of anti-particles. The universe as we know it is made up of matter, though a different choice could have been made which could have resulted in a universe made up of anti-matter.
9. Because neutrinos practically do not interact with their environment, they are difficult to observe; some scientists presume that non-luminous dark matter, which probably constitutes 90% of the mass of the universe, is made up of neutrinos.
10. Hawking, *Brief History* (n.1), 124.
11. For more information about the decoupling of the forces, see J. Silk, *The Big Bang,* New York 1989, 137–49.
12. Hawking, *Brief History* (n.1), 124.
13. Ibid., 126.
14. J. Polkinghorne, *Quarks, Chaos and Christianity*, London 1994, 29.
15. Ibid., 28.
16. Ibid., 30–1.
17. I. Barbour, *Religion in an Age of Science,* San Francisco and London 1990, 135, with reference to Hawking, *Brief History* (n.1), 128.
18. B. Carter, 'Large Number Coincidences and the Anthropic Principle in Cosmology', in M. Longair (ed.), *Confrontation of Cosmological Theories with Observation,* Dordrecht 1974, 294.
19. See J. Barrow and F. Tipler, *The Anthropic Cosmological Principle,* Oxford 1986, 108–9.
20. See Barbour, *Religion in an Age of Science* (n.17), 136–7.
21. J. Leslie, *Universes,* London and New York 1989, 15.
22. Polkinghorne, *Quarks, Chaos and Christianity* (n.14), 39–40 ; Barbour, *Religion in an Age of Science* (n.17), 173; J. L. Segundo, *Que mundo? Que hombre? Que Dios?,* Santander 1993, 419.

Creationism and Evolution

WILLEM B. DREES

According to a 1994 survey by the Social and Cultural Planning Bureau, 37% of the Dutch population believe that Adam and Eve were historical figures. Moreover 11% think that the Bible must be taken as the literal truth. 47% regard it as inspired but in the language of its time, while the rest see the Bible as a human book with old fables, legends, stories and moral codes. Evidently not all those who regard Adam and Eve as historical figures are inclined to take Genesis literally; some of them fit Adam and Eve into an evolutionary view of the world.

In the United States, by contrast, according to a 1991 Gallup Poll, 47% accepted the statement that God created human beings in their present form less than 10,000 years ago, and 40% combined an acceptance of long-term evolution with belief in God's governance. Evidently almost half the American population are open to creationist views. The number of active creationists is of course much more limited.

'Creationism' is a movement which is also not completely without significance in the Netherlands. That emerged most recently in 1995 in a discussion carried on in all the newspapers about whether or not the current theory of evolution should be included in the curriculum for the school-leaving examination. At that time the Netherlands was also host to a creationist World Congress organized by the Evangelical College in Amersfoort.

The evolution of creationism

It is sometimes thought that 'creationism' depends only on a last remnant who have not yet given up the old convictions. This picture is incorrect. Present-day creationism is the late product of a historical development; we might call it the evolution of an anti-evolutionism.

The recent form of creationism emphasizes the sudden creation of life on earth less than ten thousand years ago. Human beings and apes do not have common ancestors. Geographical strata arose above all from a world-wide inundation, the Flood. These creationists who believe in a 'young earth' have become dominant in the movement only in recent decades.

A century ago, in general the creationists accepted an old earth. Sometimes the days of Genesis 1 were interpreted as periods: after all, it says in the Psalms that for God a thousand years are like a day. Others believed that two events can be distinguished in the first chapters of Genesis, namely the creation 'in the beginning' and the creation of paradise in six days. In the period between the first and second creation, which can also be seen as a restoration, all kinds of things can have happened, including the catastrophes to which we owe the fossils. In such ways faith in the accuracy of the Bible has been combined with acceptance of the most recent geological discoveries and the finding of ancient fossils.

Not only could orthodox believers reconcile their faith with evolution; after 1859 some were even active defenders of Darwin. In the United States, the first defenders of the Darwinistic theory of evolution included the theologically orthodox botanist Asa Gray and the preacher and amateur geologist George Frederick Wright. Wright investigated the traces of the ice ages in the United States. Later, in 1912, he wrote the chapter on evolution for *The Fundamentals*, the polemical writings from which fundamentalism took its name.

Following other conservative theologians, Wright claimed that the biblical authors had known no more than their contemporaries about science, history and philosophy. The inspiration of the Bible relates to what we need to know, believe and obediently accept for our salvation. The account of the creation in Genesis is about the fact and not the manner of the divine creation. While in *The Fundamentals* he could still write that all human beings were descended from a single couple specially created by God, in 1912 we read that genetically, human beings are connected with mammals. For him evolution and a 'special creation' were not mutually exclusive. God could direct the process of evolution. So the real enemy of this movement was not evolution but the historical criticism of the Bible. Such a theistic interpretation was also generally offered in Baptist teaching establishments in the southern states.

In the 1920s there was a first 'crusade' against the theory of evolution. Biologists who accepted a theistic interpretation of the theory of evolution had problems with some of their church members. Three states forbade discussion of the theory of evolution in public schools. A biology teacher in Tennessee, John Thomas Scopes, was prosecuted in 1925 for such teaching in a public school. He was convicted of breaking the law but not punished because of a technical error. After that, publishers and authors left the theory of evolution out of school textbooks; conflicts were avoided.

A central figure in this anti-evolutionary movement and an attorney in the Scopes trial was William Jennings Bryan. His main concern was a moral one: the science that was producing deadly poison gases (which had been used in the First World War) was replacing the law of Christ with the law of the primeval forest. An anti-elitist resentment also played a role: why should a small elite of scientists determine the views of millions of American Christians? But Bryan, too, understood the days as periods: in his view, those who understand the seven days as seven periods of twenty-four hours do so to make the creationist view seem ridiculous.

By contrast, modern creationism begins from six periods of twenty-four hours. The fossils are regarded as a consequence of the flood in the time of Noah. This thesis also became established as a result of a book by John C. Whitcomb and Henry M. Morris, *The Genesis Flood (*1961), which referred back to a book by a Seventh-Day Adventist, George McCready Price's *New Geology*, 1923, that had received hardly any attention. For the Seventh-Day Adventists the seventh day, Saturday, was a day of celebration. That made them hold firmly to belief in a creation in six literal days. Moreover the leader of this movement, Ellen G. White, argued for a special interpretation of the Mosaic history of the world: the Flood and the enormous wind which followed it were a catastrophe that changed the face of the earth. The buried forests formed coal and oil (1864). Through McCready Price this 'flood geology' found a very limited following in the 1920s among conservatives.

McCready Price was asked critical questions from his own circles: why are the fossil strata, if they are not in the right order, in precisely the opposite order? If the world has been turned upside down, how can the Bible describe the world before the flood with the same rivers and mountains (Ararat) as the world afterwards? After the Scopes trial the fundamentalists attempted less to change the public schools and mainstream churches, but now formed their own network of teaching organizations, radio stations and Bible schools.

1959 marked the centenary of the appearance of Charles Darwin's *The Origin of Species*. On this occasion an article with the title '100 Years without Darwin is Enough' strongly criticized the teaching of biology in the United States, which had begun to avoid the controversial topic of evolution. Biologists began to lobby for treating their discipline from an evolutionary perspective. The status of biology had grown as a result of the unravelling of the structure and function of DNA in 1954.

In 1957 the Russians launched the unmanned Sputnik; in 1961 they led the Americans with the launching of the first manned space flight (Yuri Gagarin). So in the middle of the Cold War the Americans seemed to be getting left behind in the sphere of science and technology. This led to a state-subsidized revision of the educational system in these areas. The Biology Curriculum Project benefitted from this; an up-to-date programme of teaching was developed.

This change of climate led to resistance from parents, who were shocked at the 'atheistic' teaching of their children. The controversy was concentrated on the public schools, because the United States knows no financial equilibrium between public and private education as is the case in the Netherlands. In the Netherlands it would be cheaper for parents to withdraw into schools to their own liking.

Present-day creationism arose after this, in the 1960s. Education was not the only battlefield. In subsequent decades there was no mistaking the political role of the 'moral majority' and the influence of right-wing Christian groups. One of the best-known episodes connected with creationism took place in the state of Arkansas. A law passed there obliged biology teachers to pay as much attention to the theory of creation as to the theory of evolution. By requiring such equal treatment (instead of a fight against the theory of evolution), and by introducing both as scientific theories, it was thought that room could be made in public teaching without violating the separation of state and church laid down by the American constitution.

After being rushed through the Arkansas legislature late one afternoon, the law was challenged by teachers of biology, the Civil Rights Movement, and leaders of all the major churches and Jewish groups. In their view, by laying down a specific alternative as material to be treated, the law was violating the fundamental rule that the state cannot favour a particular religion. The judge accepted this argument: creationism was not a science but a religious conviction. The law was declared invalid.

Since then the creationists have achieved little through legislation. On the other hand, they have fought time and again at the local level, for example in the textbook committees which report on reliable or compulsory books.

To sum up, it can be said that in the course of the twentieth century the confrontation has become increasingly sharp. The theory of evolution is the focal point of discussion, but for those involved the question is one of the rejection of modern society. In this sense this is not an old phenomenon but the other side of contemporary developments.

The first arena: evolutionary biology

In creationist literature, as in the famous Arkansas trial, we find arguments of different kinds. Sometimes the discussion is scientific, sometimes it is about the nature of knowledge or faith.

First of all a brief excursus on the theory of evolution. Some giraffes have shorter necks than others. As long as a longer neck causes no specific disadvantages, long-necked giraffes are at an advantage, because they can eat more leaves from the trees. They are thus better nourished and healthier and survive times of need better; they will also have more offspring. If this condition is hereditary, there will therefore be more longer-necked than short-necked giraffes in a subsequent generation. There are of course many nuances here; thus perhaps the long neck is more of an advantage in the fight for females than in the fight for food. But this brief sketch outlines the most important elements: hereditary properties which are favourable or unfavourable in a particular environment and which therefore occur more frequently in the next generation. On this basis. the great differences in forms of life can be explained as the outcome of a long 'history of nature'.

Now a cat is more like a lion than a horse, but also more like a horse than like a fish. On the basis of such comparisons an attempt can be made to chart the great variety of forms of life. One can also research the history of being like a cat or being like a horse with the help of fossils, and thus produce a 'genealogy'. Finally, one can looked at the protein and DNA in different organisms and in this way arrive at genealogies. In my view the strongest argument for the evolutionary approach is that anatomical similarity, fossil forms of life and DNA research lead to the same genealogy.

Creationists often refer to the missing pieces in the puzzle, so-called 'missing links', in the fossil chain. Of course the puzzle is incomplete, since it is a reconstruction of history. But time and again pieces of the puzzle are found. Thus some years ago in Pakistan a fossil whale was found with small feet, a link between present-day whales and previous land-dwellers. Moreover creationists claim that the complexity of living organisms is too great for them to have arisen through evolution. That something like a living cell has arisen by chance, by the right ingredients being shaken together long enough, is infinitesimally small – as if a wind blowing through a scrap heap could build a Boeing.

But evolution works with very many small steps and that makes a big difference. Imagine two clockmakers in a city, Horus and Tempus. Both build splendid clocks from thousands of pieces. They become famous, and demand for their clocks constantly increases. Horus builds his clocks in one continuous process; if he has to stop work, everything falls apart and he has to begin again. By contrast, Tempus builds smaller units, each made up of ten elements, and then combines these into parts each of a hundred elements; with these he builds the clock. Horus gets behind, the more customers come into the shop, and produces nothing. It is extremely difficult to build such a complex thing all at once. But evolution works with many small steps. In such a way a great deal is possible: the whole rich variety of life on our planet.

The second arena: the philosophy of science

Discussion about creationism and evolution has also been carried on with arguments from the philosophy of science. Science is about theories; these are always provisional. Evolution, too, is only a theory and is not absolutely certain. So wouldn't it be a good thing also to try out another theory? Therefore, one Dutch parliamentarian argues, both creationism and evolution should be treated on an equal level in teaching.

Now the word 'theory' is used in different ways. At times it means that something is merely an intellectual construction, and has to prove its worth in practice, an idea for which there are as yet no good arguments. At times the term is used in a wider sense: for example, 'theory' is a notion and not a thing. Thus the view that the earth is flat and the view that it is almost a sphere are each called 'theory'. Nevertheless they are not to be taken equally seriously. For good reasons – confirmed every day by air travel and international trade – we assume that the theory that the earth is a sphere is correct; and this is taught in schools. So too the theory of evolution is a theory, a view of reality formulated by human beings, but it is not 'just theory', for which there are no good arguments.

People are fond of claiming that the theory of evolution cannot be refuted and therefore is unscientific: biologists are said to tell stories about the chance nature of all phenomena. But that is not correct. Rather, the theory of evolution would come up against considerable problems if the geologists had to explain, say, that there had been life on earth only for a few thousand years, of if we suddenly found in the earth from the pre-Cambrian period, i.e. a time when there was as yet no multi-cellular life, fossils of human species or other vertebrates.

The religious arena

In the end, those engaging in this polemic are not concerned with the theory of evolution but with the Bible and the values of family and society, which in their view are at risk. But in my view creationism also fails seriously in this arena.

At the time of Charles Darwin, Philip H. Gosse wrote the book *Omphalos* (navel). Among other things he raised the question whether Adam had a navel. As the first human being he had no mother and therefore also no umbilical cord, but without a navel he would be different from other human beings. Another question is this. We can see from tree rings how old the trees are. Did the trees in paradise really have rings? Gosse said yes: God created the trees with tree rings and Adam with a navel; God created reality with all the signs of a lengthy past. This solution is logically compelling, but makes science an absurd activity. Astronomers and geologists would be analysing an illusion. Nor would that be a gain for faith: God would appear as the great conjurer, if not as a cheat.

So creationism means the repudiation of science and thus the repudiation of God's gifts, both the gifts of human curiosity and intelligence and the gifts of the world with its regularities and its accidents. Such a belief rejects creation as we have come to know it through the natural sciences, God comes to be opposed to nature.

In conclusion I would like to indicate briefly two alternatives here. The first is about the way in which we read the Bible. In the discussion about the place of the earth and the sun Galileo Galilei quoted a cardinal who is said to have remarked that the Bible did not seek to tell us how the heavens go, but about how we go to heaven. So it could be said that the question is not how life came into being, but how we should live. The function of religious language differs from that of scientific language.

Secondly, in the view of reality one could also attempt to see the natural as God's work. God is the ground of existence; the ground also of regularities and chance, which has led to this rich variety of forms of life. The Anglican priest and biochemist Arthur Peacocke used the image of the composer: just as Beethoven is present to us in music, so God is present in the world. Or one could think of a musician improvising, who plays on developing forms in reality. God is not a God who works only in the gaps which the sciences leave open; rather, God is the ground and creator of this event. How can we imagine everything? To answer that question would take more time and space than is available here. But the quest for a comprehensive explanation (instead of the creationist repudiation of it) seems to me to be a worthier way for both human beings and God to deal with one another, reality and our knowledge.

Translated by John Bowden

Select bibliography

On evolution

Richard Dawkins, *The Blind Watchmaker*, Harlow 1986
Daniel D. Dennett, *Darwin's Dangerous Idea*, New York 1995
Tijs Goldschmidt, *Darwins hoofdvijver*, Amsterdam 1995

On creationism

C. J. Houtman et al., *Schepping of evolutie: Het creationisme een alternatif?*, Kampen 1986
Philip Kitchen, *Abusing Science: The Case against Creationism*, Cambridge, Mass. 1982
Ronald L. Numbers, *The Creationists: The Evolution of Scientific Creationism*, Berkeley 1993

On theology and evolution

Philip Hefner, *The Human Factor: Evolution, Culture and Religion*, London 1993
Arthur Peacocke, *Theology for a Scientific Age*, London 1993

Process Theology and Evolution

MARJORIE H. SUCHOCKI

How does the use of process philosophy facilitate a Christian theology of an evolutionary creation? In order to address this question, I briefly summarize some of the main points of the philosophy, and its utilization by biologists in evolution theory. This becomes the basis for suggesting a Christian doctrine of God as Creator, and the world as creation.

Process theology, utilizing the cosmology of Alfred North Whitehead, has engaged in conversation with the sciences from its very inception. Whitehead himself was a mathematician and physicist who turned to philosophy in order to answer the question, 'What must the structure of the world be like if quantum physics is descriptive of reality?' His answer in the formidable *Process and Reality*[1] posits a dynamic universe that is continuously constructed by successive 'actual entities', droplets of experience, constituted by their internal relations. In Whitehead's model, each instant of becoming inherits the energies of its past, integrates them into itself in the light of its own purposes, and becomes a datum for its successors, who repeat the process. Always, the transmission of energy is a movement from past to present in an internalized experience 'here' of what happened 'there', and a movement from present to future as the newly created fact evokes successors who will include its influence in their own becoming. Thus at its most basic level, reality is both subject and object. It is a subject in that the occasion experiences the influences of the past and decisively integrates them; it is an object in that, once its integration is complete, it becomes datum for its successor.

I. God's immanence in the world

Thus far, even in this highly abbreviated description of process thought, one might see its relationship to the sciences, particularly that of biology. If every occasion succeeds its past by integrating that past in some novel way within itself, we have the makings of an evolutionary world. But my 'thumbnail sketch' requires a further elaboration in order to indicate the value of process philosophy for theological reflection in general, and for a theology of creation in particular.

Whitehead was committed to the principle of coherence. He wanted to provide a general system of thought that accounted for 'the way of things' without irrational leaps. Thus he held it as axiomatic that the reasons for things must finally be rooted in actual entities. But in his account, an occasion's integration of the past could not possibly be a simple repetition of the past, because no occasion in that past had to integrate exactly the same past. 'The many become one, and are increased by one.'[2] The past is always being added to by the present, which means that the past is, in some sense, always newly configured. There is a principle of novelty at work in the world, resting within the freedom of each occasion as it integrates its past. What is the source of this novelty? This conundrum led Whitehead to posit a relational God, source of novelty, ever interacting with the world.

For theology, of course, such a model of God provided new resources for appropriating biblical notions of a covenantal God who influences and responds to the world in every instant of its becoming. Whitehead's technical language described a God who gives an 'initial aim' to each becoming instant, with this initial aim offering guidance for how to integrate the past. This provided a precise language for talking about God's immanence in the world, even as the notion of God as source of all possibility gave a language for talking about God's transcendence of the world. Process theologians drew upon the philosophical insights to give fresh form to biblical and traditional expressions of faith.

But process philosophy has proved useful for scientists as well as for theologians. Process denies that we exist in a mechanistic world, where evolution proceeds only by external effects upon otherwise inert particles of organisms. Because reality is dynamic, we can posit three forms of causation: efficient causation, which refers to the stubborn facticity of an occasion's past as it influences the present; final causation, which refers to God's provision of an aim toward how the occasion might become given this particular past; and self-causation, which refers to the way the becoming occasion, in its own subjectivity, weaves these two forms of causation together. Self-constitution is the foundation of freedom.[3] As the Australian biologist Charles Birch notes, it is also the basis for the affirmation of a principle formulated by Charles Kingsley in his classic novel, *The Water Babies*, that God makes things that make themselves.[4]

II. Self-organization and saltation

Evolutionary theory encounters two issues that are irresolvable in a totally mechanistic world.[4] The first is self-organization, and the second is saltation, or apparent leaps of discontinuity in and among species. Self-organization is the peculiar ability of some organisms to coalesce without any central authority. Charles Birch cites the example of a simple tobacco virus in which all the pans are complexly ordered. If the virus is split apart, it spontaneously reassembles.[5] How does it 'know' to do this? Another example is the termite. There is no 'master architect' in the termite world; the termite we have named 'queen' is more like an incubator than a ruler. Yet termites build exceedingly complex structures, simply through local interactions among thousands of termites. This is self-organization. A mechanistic model of the world cannot account for this action, but a dynamic world, where each microscopic component responds to its feelings of its environments is a world where self-organization should be expected.

Saltation, or dramatic discontinuity, is also a problem in evolutionary theory. David Griffin reviews a large number of situations where the gradualism of natural selection seems inadequate to account for the fossil evidence. On the contrary, fossil remains seem to indicate great leaps within a geologically brief period of time. For example, there is no easy explanation for the radical differences between the blob of jelly that constitutes the egg of a frog or fish and an amniotic egg. Also, if birds evolved from reptiles, as is supposed, there is no account of how an intermediate creature, with scales becoming feathers, could possibly have survived. In these and many other cases, the gaps between species seem far too large to be explained through the gradualism of natural selection alone.

But if, in addition to feelings of the past, becoming occasions are also affected by a lure towards novelty, then apparent discontinuity could occur. What would be required, says Griffin, is several steps. First, there must be a succession of occasions whose context allows them to receive a novel aim from God toward greater complexity, even though the environment does not yet support that type of complexity. This aim, while not yet possible for full actualization, would be entertained as a datum in the mental pole of the occasion. Eventually, an environment is produced where a successor occasion can actualize the novel datum received through the cumulative past and through its own immediate aim from God. This produces a change in the internal constitution of the occasion that affects its own successors, who may now feel the effect of that datum physically as well as mentally. A process called 'canalization' then happens, which 'suddenly' produces the radical change. The suddenness, of course, is appearance only, for the actual process would have been at work in countless generations of predecessors. The point is that in a dynamic world of internal relations, where influence is received from the environment (the past) and from God (as a future), discontinuities are natural.

Another aspect of evolutionary theory that is puzzling is the 'Cambrian explosion' that occurred following a long period of stasis. The Cambrian period lasted roughly ten million years – a short amount of time in evolutionary terms. Natural selection alone has difficulty in accounting for the burst of creative activity that resulted in the origins of most of the animal kingdom during this period in time. But if natural selection is incorporated within the wider view of causation given in the above process explanation dealing with saltation, the activity of the Cambrian period is understandable.[6]

These comments are just bare indications of how process-oriented biologists and philosophers of science supplement Darwinian theories in order better to understand the evolution of life in our world.[7] Darwin's genius provided the initial mechanism by which we could begin to gain a more adequate understanding of ourselves and our world, but the fossil record and the observed behaviours of organisms require that we substitute a doctrine of internal relations for the Darwinian supposition of external relations.

III. God's call of God

This brief survey provides background for the development of a process theology of creation.[8] In the light of this account, it should be apparent that to read the majestic first chapter of Genesis through 'process eyes' is to see a remarkable portrayal of creation through evolution. The text begins with suggestions of chaos rather than with the notion of *creatio ex nihilo* that has been read into the text. From an evolutionary point of view, of course – and from a process point of view – this is an apt beginning. As David Griffin points out, a situation of chaos is one where there is no observable order of inheritance from any organized past; hence the influence of the past on the present is minimal.[9] The influence from God, then, is correspondingly strong, so that rapid and divinely induced change can endure. But even under such conditions, God does not act unilaterally. The finite occasions of the world must respond to the divine aims if in fact those aims are to be accomplished.

And the text suggests just such a situation. God broods over the chaos, then utters a command: 'Let there be light!' Creation is through a word, a call, a lure towards a particular form of becoming. Creation responds. There is light. The light is itself an introduction of difference and therefore definition into the chaos. If there is 'light' and 'dark', then there is a form of order. Self-organization theory is suggestive, for we can envision vast numbers of occasions interacting with one another, each of which has received a similar divine lure. In so far as occasions respond to the lure of 'lightness', the possibility of lightness begins to become embodied, creating a past that adds its own influence to that of God's aim for the successor occasions. It would be like the dawn of creation, with light intensifying in continuous response to God's call.

C. S. Lewis has written a children's story, *The Magician's Nephew,* in which he gives a memorable image of God's creating power. The Lion, Aslan, is Lewis' symbol of the Word of God. A child who has fallen into the newly beginning universe of Narnia hears a voice singing in the darkness; it is the Lion, singing creation into being. The child watches and listens in awe, for the form of the Lion becomes visible in the newly dawning light. As the long, continuous note of the song resounds, the light grows, until finally the full light of day has appeared. Even so in a process interpretation of Genesis 1: God calls, and the world responds by becoming itself.

But the texts offer even more. God calls, and the world responds, but then God responds to the world with judgment, valuation: 'and God saw that the light was good.' This is no 'clockmaker' deistic God, impassively spinning a world into space. Instead we have a God who responds to the world evaluatively and actively, building on this response with the next divine action. We have a responsive God interacting with the world, calling it into being, responding to it, and calling it into being yet again. This is a God for whom the act of creating is itself a form of covenant; it is creation through call and response.

Note also the progressive nature of the text. The sequencing of events is intentional, for each action builds towards the possibility of the next. That is, light, dark, and a world of ocean and dry land is necessary for the possibility of vegetation, and vegetation is necessary for the possibility of animal life. This is not an 'all at once' creation; it is progressive, with the cumulative past providing the ever-new context in which the next stage of 'call and response' can occur. God's call depends upon creaturely response, and on the divine response to what the creature has done with the divine call. Given 'that', 'this' is now possible. This is theistic evolution; it is also a process commentary on the dynamism of the Genesis text.

That the Genesis text speaks of 'days' is not problematical. The language of the text is tensive, liturgical and 'thick' in nuance. It is not reducible to the mundanities of a television news report. Its nearest parallel in the biblical witness is the Psalms: Psalm 148, for instance, is a repetition of Genesis 1 in the context of praise. Genesis 1 gives its narrative from the divine perspective, and Psalm 148 repeats the narrative from the creation's perspective. Joy, gratitude and a delight in being pervade creation in response to the Creator's call, with all creation unified in the praise of God. The psalm and the Genesis text match each other in liturgical wonder, and the point of Genesis is not to set one's clock, but to set one's heart responsively to the call of one's Creator.

IV. World's free response

God's call enables a particular response to take place, but it does not determine that response. As the world grows in complexity, that initial period where chaos offered little resistance to the divine call was naturally replaced with billions of canalizations creating a cumulative past that also affects the response of each becoming entity. Just as in the Genesis text the earlier creative response affects what the next divine call will be, even so the growing complexity of creation affects the divine call. God's aims to us are contextual, giving us possibilities in the light of the particular past. And the actualization of God's aims depends upon the free response of the world. Each entity balances the strength of its past in relation to God's call to its future; there is no necessity for it to respond positively to God's call. When, in fact, the cumulative responses have negated God's calls, the continuing aims are correspondingly affected. What is really possible is conditioned by the past. A 'call and response' creation allows evil as well as good.

The Christian tradition asserts in its doxology, 'As it was in the beginning, is now and ever shall be, world without end!' This is deeply affirmed by a process theology of creation, for we maintain that God is *always* Creator, and always Creator through call and response. It is not that once, aeons ago, God created in the way portrayed in Genesis and then stopped. Rather, God continues to create through call and response, touching every becoming entity with a lure toward its best integration of its past. Thus a process theology of creation is also a theology of providence, describing the dynamics of God's contemporary work with the world. Creation is a continuous activity, applicable throughout time, always present.

I have indicated that God responds to the world's response, and that God's response issues into the shaping of each new aim for every becoming aspect of existence. But it must also be noted that God's response to the world is posited as an internalized response. That is, just as creation integrates the divine call into its own becoming, even so God integrates the resulting world into God's own becoming. It matters to God what happens in the world, for God receives the world. Again, just as it rests with each creaturely occasion to respond as it will to what ii has received, even so, it rests with the divine will how to integrate the world into the divine life. Thus a doctrine of creation as call and response also entails an eschatology, a doctrine of judgement and redemption.[10]

Finally, to discuss an evolutionary theology of creation from a process perspective requires some attention to purpose. Many biologists find the notion of purpose problematic relative to evolution. They point to the many dead ends in evolution, and to the long aeons of stasis for some species, such as sharks. There is also the reversion from complexity to simplicity, as occurs in some intestinal parasites which rely more and more on their hosts' natural functions to replace their own. Evolution is not a steady-state process of progress from simplicity to complexity. On these grounds, purpose is thoroughly denied.[11] In human experience, then, purpose is an anomaly in the world, without parallel in the natural order.

Because of its understanding of internal relations, a process theology of creation must refute this view. Indeed, it takes the human experience of purpose to be a highly sophisticated development of an intentionality that pervades all nature. Philosophically, purpose is grounded in the requirement that every occasion must integrate its past toward a feeling of what it can become; this is a rudimentary form of purpose. It is mediated to each occasion through the initial aim received from God. Theologically, this means that God's interactions with the world are purposive.

While it is quite the case that no species necessarily advances, and all species eventually suffer extinction, these facts do not contradict purpose. Purpose must be considered on three levels: the microscopic level of what happens to each actual entity, the macroscopic level of what happens to successive organizations of entities in the becoming world, and the divine level.

Microscopically, each occasion of experience aims towards its own becoming, with some appetition that its becoming shall have an effect beyond itself (which it does, of course, in at least the next generation of succeeding occasions). Metaphysically, then, its own becoming is its accomplishment of its own internal purpose. Since the model of an actual occasion of experience is intended to suggest the dynamics somewhere at the level of the quark, clearly there are billions and billions of occasions, each satisfying its own purpose for becoming. A universe of internal relations is rife with purpose.

Macroscopically, routes of inheritance are formed. Given the vast number of occasions in the universe, clearly there are also a vast number of routes of inheritance, each with its own cumulative purpose. In every case, God deals with these routes one member at a time, offering possibilities for each one that will create a particular context for the many. We must speak of purposes, in the plural, not of 'purpose'. In the very nature of the case most of these purposes are unknown to us.

But we do know of one particular route: the movement from simplicity to complexity that has occurred which describes the macro-world in which we live, and indeed our own selves. Theologically, the call and response of the creative God has led 'from the cell to the community', to quote from the title of the Birch/Cobb book mentioned previously. We posit that we are not 'done' yet; that God continues to call us to deeper and richer forms of community; and that most of this purposive call is mediated through religious communities. Human evolution continues.

And there is yet the overarching purpose of God's own self. Philosophically, process thought speaks of God's aim toward intensity of experience, which is the richness of many contrasts held together in a unity of experience. Theologically, this is the aim toward communities with ever-increasing concerns for well-being, both within and beyond each community's borders. We are called to be a world community of communities of caring, of justness. To be so is to know the richness of contrasts that do not lead to destruction, but to life.

If God draws at least the world of humans towards such a becoming, then this says something about God's own purposes. If God is a God who creates through call and response, and if God also experiences internal relations, then God is affected by the world's response to God. God not only utilizes the world's response to fashion new aims for the ever-becoming world, but God utilizes the world's response within the depths of the divine nature – evaluating the world, judging the world, redeeming the world through its participation in God's own life. God is the destiny of the world and the final purpose of the world.

A process theology of creation, then, far from finding evolution a challenge or an obstacle to a doctrine of creation, uses evolution to deepen its understanding of creation as call and response. The world is formed in and through its response to God, not only 'in the beginning' but today and tomorrow as well. The God of creation is the God of providence, and the God of providence is the God or out destiny.

Notes

1. A. N. Whitehead, *Process and Reality, An Essay in Cosmology,* corrected edition, ed. David Ray Griffin and Donald W. Sherburne, New York 1978; original New York 1929, 21.
2. Ibid.
3. Charles Birch, 'Processing Towards Life', *Process Studies* 27/3–4, 286. Birch is arguably the foremost biologist using process thought to further the scientific study of evolution. See his *On Purpose,* Kensington, New South Wales 1990.
4. Volume 27/3–4 of the journal *Process Studies* contains six articles relating process philosophy to evolution. Authors of these articles are Jay Schulkin, Research Professor of Physiology and Biophysics at Georgetown University; A. Karim Ahmed, Deputy Director of Health, Environment and Development at World Resources Institute; Joseph Early, Professor of Chemistry at Georgetown University; Charles Birch, Professor Emeritus (Biology), University of Sydney; Granville C. Henry and Robert J. Valenza, both Professors of Mathematics at Claremont McKenna College.
5. Birch, 'Processing Towards Life' (n.3), 281.
6. David Griffin, *Religion and Scientific Naturalism: Overcoming the Conflicts,* unpublished manuscript scheduled for publication by State University of New York Press in 2000.
7. For a fuller development see Charles Birch, *On Purpose* (n.3).
8. There are several book-length treatments of a process theology of evolutionary creation. See Richard Overman, *Evolution and the Christian Doctrine of Creation: A Whiteheadian Interpretation,* Philadelphia 1967; Charles Birch and John B. Cobb, Jr, *The Liberation of Life: From Cell to the Community,* Denton 1990; Jerry Korsmeyer, *Evolution and Eden: Balancing Original Sin and Contemporary Science,* New Jersey 1998; and David Ray Griffin's forthcoming book, *Religion and Scientific Naturalism* (n.6).
9. Griffin, *Religion and Scientific Naturalism* (n.6).
10. I have developed these notions in three books: *God, Christ, Church: A Practical Guide to Process Theology,* revised edition, New York 1989; *The End of Evil. Process Eschatology in Historical Context,* Albany 1988; and *The Fall of Violence: Original Sin in Relational Theology,* New York 1994.
11. See, for example, the many writings of Stephen Gould, such as *Life's Grandeur,* London 1996.

‘The Lord and Giver of Life’. Towards a Theology of ‘Life’

CHRISTOPH THEOBALD

A quick look at the Niceno–Constantinopolitan creed shows us that the term ‘life’ occurs in it in two different places, first to characterize the creative activity of the Holy Spirit, ‘giver of life’ (*zōopoios*), and a second time to denote what believers expect: ‘the resurrection of the dead and the life (*zōēn*) of the world to come’. In the tradition, believers expect ‘the resurrection of the dead and life’ (initially two different places). So it was necessary to wait until the 1960s to find alongside traditional dictionary articles on ‘eternal life’ others which dealt with just ‘life’. Probably the work of the ‘life-giving (*zōopoios*) Spirit’ was assimilated too quickly to that of the ‘Creator (*poiētēs*) of heaven and earth, of all things visible and invisible, who is mentioned in the first article of the creed. Today we can see more clearly the consequences of the void left in the theology of creation by this monotheistic reduction and the parallel imposition of the causal model in its totality.

Now according to the biblical economy it is quite decisive to begin from ‘life’ and never separate it from its eschatological orientation, which is clearly expressed in many ways. From Genesis to the Apocalypse God himself proves to be ‘the Living One’ in person, freely giving access to the tree of life, not to mention the very source of living water. It is not only death which opposes life – a banal observation to make – but death *and* the lie, which are inextricably intertwined. In fact everything takes place as if death obtained its power over life only by suggesting to human beings a secret connivance between the inherent limits to their lives and an underlying jealousy, thus provoking in turn a defensive reaction, indeed a relentless struggle to obtain it, often to the detriment of others. Only ‘The Living One’ himself could thus get to the end of this lie which is so stamped on humankind and root in us trust in him as a gratuitous superabundance of life, which extends to its very limits.

But what if this faith were itself an imposture, disguising the tragic ruse of a life which overwhelms us from all sides, capable of exploiting individuals with their inexorable limitations for its own endless propagation? Isn't that what common sense teaches us, not to mention the results of scientific research? At all times – from the wise men of the Bible to current debates between theologians and biologists, via the revival of Hellenistic philosophy among the Fathers, the concept of life has been exposed to a controversy in which ultimately the understanding and the very approach of death is at stake. It is enough here to recall the decisive work of Gregory of Nyssa who, at the time of the composition of the creed and in the footsteps of Plato and Plotinus, identifies 'life' and 'desire' (*epithumia),* while emphasizing with the biblical tradition the understanding and the very approach of death. We need only recall the celebrated passage from the *Life of Moses* on the desire to see God (Ex. 33.20). He writes:

> You will not be able to see my face. No man may see my face without dying. Scripture does not tell us that in the sense that this sight could become the cause of the death of those who enjoy it. How could the face of Life ever be the cause of death for those who approach it? But since the divine Being is life-giving (*zōopoion*) in essence, and on the other hand the distinctive character of the divine nature is being beyond all determination, the one who thinks that God is some determined thing misses the one who is Being in essence, and grasps what the subjective activity of the mind takes for being, and does not have Life. For true Life is that which is so in essence. Now this essence is inaccessible to knowledge . . . What Moses desires – to see the face of life – he thus accomplishes for himself by himself, so that his desire remains unquenched.

This experience of a desire for life that is never quenched, which runs in a remarkable continuity throughout the whole of creation to take root there, beyond the limits of death, in the Living One himself, is no longer immediately accessible in a vision of the world stamped by contemporary biology and its concept of life, 'secularized' and based on radical contingency. So it is necessary to do the work of Gregory of Nyssa and a whole tradition all over again. Therefore here I shall first look quickly at the epistemological conditions for a critical articulation of the approaches of biology and theology. After that I shall reflect on the concept of 'life' and its two aspects, terrestrial and eschatological, ending by pointing out some elements of a 'spirituality' of life.

I. A plea for a model of critical articulation

Science and myth

First let us recall that in recent years the classical frontier between science and myth has again become mobile. Certainly in order to give themselves a scientific status, the life sciences had to struggle against anthropomorphism throughout the nineteenth century. How was it possible not to make use of *purpose,* which characterizes so many human activities, as a universal model to explain everything in nature that seems orientated on an end and argue from the evident usefulness of all the organs of a living being to the intention of a creator? Now Darwin shows how the combination of three simple conditions explains the simulation of a pre-established design: it is enough for the fundamental structures of life to vary, for them to be hereditary, and for the reproduction of certain variants to be favoured by the milieu. So the notion of *natural selection* comes out on top. It gives, so to speak, a change of direction and orientates the play of variations which arise by chance, producing increasingly complex wholes, adjusted over millions of years in response to the challenges of the environment. Darwin already had to defend himself against the resurgence of anthropomorphism which consisted in making selection a natural force. And more recently Stephen J. Gould has opposed an 'adaptionist' interpretation of the theory of evolution which gives natural selection the power of being an optimizing agent and neglects a whole series of constraints – morphological, for example – which in no way depend on adaptation to the milieu. By reducing living organisms to characters or structures, each of which fulfils a function in the best way possible, one ends up constructing what Gould calls a 'Panglossian universe', taking the name of Voltaire's famous doctor, who explains to his pupil Candide that it is impossible for things to be other than they are, 'for everything is good'.

However, while constantly struggling against anthropomorphism, today biology must recognize (along with microphysics) that it cannot put itself outside the relationship between the observer and the observed. Even its basic concepts, for example that of the 'genetic programme', are metaphors. Certainly these have a considerable heuristic and operational value, but they lose that when it is forgotten that they are metaphors which denote mechanisms of which we are ignorant. Furthermore, as soon as one seeks to bring together the enormous number of facts in a kind of 'natural history', one is obliged to appeal to the cinematic concept of the *scenario*. As F. Jacob writes:

> It is not certain that one can ever know how living beings emerged from an inert universe. Nor that one can ever understand the evolution of the brain and the appearance of the collection of properties which we find difficult to define but which we call thought. Any attempt to describe the evolution of the brain and the mind can therefore only be a simple story, a *scenario*.

The theory of evolution, which no one contests any longer in its entirety, in fact has a particular status: less because it covers mechanisms that we do not yet know or because it gives rise to different interpretations (as was suggested above), but above all because its global status makes it akin to myth. Has it not served, and does it not still serve – for instance in the framework of sociobiology – to explain all the cosmological, biological, cultural, not to say moral, transformations of our world? Even if these abusive extensions have been rejected, it cannot be denied that the theory of evolution introduces observers and their need of coherence and desire to give meaning to their own existence in the universe.

It is here in fact that the specific nature of contemporary biology emerges, opposed as it is to any idea of predetermined design or to any arguments from effect to cause. It is based on the radical contingency of variations in the structure and form of life, which can be, cannot be or also can be in quite a different way, a contingency which affects not only the manifestation of life in all its degrees and at every moment, but also observers and their perspectives. The explanatory coherence established by the researcher can therefore never free itself from this bond to 'historical' contingencies which are orientated on a retrospective approach, capable of modification each time the perspective of the observer changes. This explanatory approach obeys the 'reductionist paradigm' to the degree that the sciences cannot not not reduce the semblance of purpose to a minimum of basic mechanisms; but they also know that they avoid the myth of the power of natural selection only if they constantly allow themselves to be presented with questions arising out of the complexity of the systems and the scales of observation and comprehension.

A model of critical articulation

Theologians have a considerable interest in noting these epistemological conditions of the theory of evolution and relating to them critically through their own approach to 'life'. If the desire of nineteenth-century biology simply to substitute its theory of evolution for the creationist interpretation of reality produced either a reaction of rejection (*conflict model* or refusal to articulate) on the part of Christians, or, notably in Protestant theology, a renewed emphasis on the difference between the perspective of science and faith (*independence model*), the new sensitivity of the sciences to the particular – quasi-mythical – status of the theory of evolution prompted numerous attempts at synthesis between the scientific approach and the 'spiritual' interpretation of the history of nature and life (convergence model). The work of Teilhard de Chardin and also the process theology inspired by Whitehead or Moltmann's *God in Creation* (1985), sub-titled 'An Ecological Doctrine of Creation', draw on this model of integration (which the Tübingen theologian goes on to call a perichoretic model). From the scientific side, we observe in Princeton Gnosis (1969), in popularizers like P. Davies, F. Capra and other New Age writers, a growing interest in Asian spiritualities with their 'holistic' conceptions of the universe, hardly sensitive to the struggles between faith and science which have marked the history of European modernity. On what basis does one object to Asians who integrate the sciences, which came into being in the Graeco–Judaeo–Christian world, into their own cultural area? And is it not obvious that the globalization of all these exchanges encourages a radical pluralism which is perfectly integrated into a global consciousness that takes account of a divine – whether empty or full hardly matters – and in any case the origin and end of the infinite varieties of life?

However, it has to be noted that scientists are not knowledgeable enough about the religious sources to which they refer. This produces in them, but also (conversely) in the theologians of the convergence model, important conceptual shifts, whether this is Teilhard's ontological and theological use of the fundamental law of complexity–consciousness or the identification of the subatomic movement with the dance of Shiva, or even the transition from cyclical models of evolution to the cycle of the Upanishads in others. The metaphorical status of a certain number of basic concepts of biology threatens to disappear at the expense of an extensive and mythical concept of the evolution of life, which finally deprives itself of any possibility of criticism. These are basically the conditions of writing a 'narrative' of the history of life which those who adopt the convergence model leave in the shade, thinking that their holism functions without presuppositions.

At all events, it seems to me that Christian theology finds itself more at ease in *a model of critical articulation* which takes account simultaneously on the one hand of the difference between the scientific approaches to life and the articulation of them and on the other the human postulation of meaning.

The act of faith and the giving of meaning do not belong to the order of representation. When the mother in II Maccabees addresses her sons who are preparing to suffer martyrdom, she acknowledges her ignorance of the origin of life: 'I do not know how you came into being in my womb. It was not I who gave you life and breath, nor I who set in order the elements within each of you. Therefore the creator of the world, who shaped the beginning of man and devised the origin of all things, will in his mercy give life and breath back to you again, since you now forget yourselves for the sake of the laws' (II Macc. 7.22ff.). But it must also be added that *there is no act of faith without anthropomorphic representations,* as is again shown by the words of the mother – mobile and plural representations depending on traditions and cultures. However, that does not mean that all these representations are valid, that all are compatible with the act of faith: *that is so to speak at work within the very heart of our images of life.* So it is not difficult to show that the life sciences have led Christian exegesis and theology in modernity towards the double *theologal* awareness of the impossibility of grasping the character of the *origin* of life (not to be confused with its beginning) and the necessarily anthropomorphic status of all 'creation stories'. But conversely, the presence of the Christian faith and that of other traditions and postulations of meaning in our society send science back to its own convictions, inviting it not to delete from its account of evolution its always distinctive standpoints, which at all events are rooted in its freedom to give meaning. This mutual questioning between scientists and theologians, which presupposes the capacity of self-criticism on both sides, is the true strength of the model of critical articulation.

In the last instance this model requires theologians and researchers, each from their own perspective, to reflect *on the anthropomorphic status of the concept of life*: we are *inevitably* situated *in* human life. It is this limit which constitutes us, but to recognize it as a limit is an act of thought which has already gone beyond it; in this going beyond we have both our unrepresentable relationship to the origin ('I do not know how . . .') and – in another order – the attempt of the sciences to transcend our imagination and arrive at the very mechanisms of life. From the theological side, anthropomorphism is both honoured and surpassed by the paradoxical affirmation of the creation of life by the Living One *ex nihilo* (II Macc. 7.28): the whole of life comes only from God; it is the trace of a free gift. Now the nature of the gift is that it hides the donor, on pain of putting an obligation on the recipient and destroying what characterizes the gift: the fact that it is absolutely gratuitous. From a theological perspective, the anthropomorphism of the narratives about the origin of life signifies that it is impossible to talk of the whole of life in an 'objective' way, abstracting the human being who freely gives meaning to the origin of life. How could one recognize the creation of life without making it in the very form of every gift, which is freedom? *In scientific circles* this treatment of anthropomorphism is not unacceptable, provided that it is thought of in terms of the postulation of a meaning'. Two basic rules seem to characterize this.

Regulating the 'postulation of meaning'

1. At the final point of their mediation, most scientists who reflect on the evolution of life link up with different approaches, scientific, aesthetic, metaphysical and possibly religious; they link up with them, i.e. they join them, since at these decisive moments when the issue is one of meaning, it is no longer some anonymous science which speaks but the scientist in person. To respect the rights of criticism to the end requires that the 'thresholds' between the different 'levels' of an itinerary of meaning are well marked.

The transition from one order to another is never a 'necessary' one. No one is obliged, for example, to interpret the chance emergence of human life (with its initial conditions which are so precise) as a ruse of genes, as a first manifestation of the tragedy of life, or again as a promise. It is precisely here that the freedom of researchers to give meaning to their own existence in the universe comes in.

Since it is non-necessary, the transition from one level of discourse to another is not arbitrary or purely irrational. Everything in fact takes place as if the level of the discourse about meaning had left 'traces' (or 'limits') at the level of the scientific discourse: these present themselves in the form of 'problems', 'aporias' or 'questions'. Again it is necessary to know how to find them: it is one thing to analyse the structures of genes with the help of the concept of information, and another to see that forgetfulness of the metaphorical status of this concept already involves a 'preformationist' interpretation of the whole of the genetic and epigenetic process, a philosophical interpretation which is certainly not the only one possible. It is probably necessary already to have reflected on science as a human act which is both individual and social to become sensitive to this subtle interweaving of the scientific approach and philosophical questioning. It could be said that it is necessary already to have passed to the level of the discourse about meaning to be capable of discovering its traces at the heart of a discourse about the history of the biosphere and geosphere.

Is it clear at what point this articulation of different types of approaches obeys a complex logic? In fact it combines the non-necessary mode with the non-arbitrary mode of the transition from one level to another, thus connecting an intellectual treatment which has its starting point in scientific discourse with another which begins from the human fact of the postulation of a meaning. There are several ways of understanding the complex status of statements which relate simultaneously to the sciences and to the humane 'sciences' or philosophy: the notion of 'trace' takes us from the rational mode of a scientific explanation of things to that of the interpretation of texts, the two being connected by the famous 'hermeneutical circle'. To mark aporias or questions on the first arc of the circle – which begins from the universe to explain the emergence of life – already presupposes the second arc of the circle, which begins from human beings and their freedom to give meaning to their existence by interpreting the traces of meaning which are presented by the emergence of life (or their absence). The metaphor of the circle well indicates the mutual conditioning of these two intellectual and spiritual circles. The risk of the vicious circle is avoided by the impossibility of stopping the circulation once and for all, since each of the two approaches is continually relaunched by the other.

2. The first rule of the giving of meaning thus relates to the correct articulation of the different intellectual approaches involved in this act, the point being to guarantee its freedom (its non-necessary or non-arbitrary modality), without which there can be no meaning. A second rule relates to the form of the discourse about meaning. This is the meaning expressed in a narrative. Why? Because to speak of the meaning of life in the universe, of human life in particular, is to engage in its historic destiny; it is to trace a way which goes from its beginning to its end, and this is an impossible task without telling a story, without composing narratives: as it goes on, the discourse on meaning tends in fact to take up a position in relation to the totality of the real.

This apparently exorbitant statement takes us back to the question of the relationship between science and myth which I have already touched on. Several indications which have already been noted make us cautious about too rigorous a separation of the domains which threatens to reduce the reign of meaning to some episodes of human history. Where are we to seek the reason for this apparently inevitable link between scientific discourse about life and the narrative of a natural and human history? It is given us by the notion of *trace*, as we have already noted in connection with the first rule. Its mixed status destines it to play a mediating role: it relates to the marking or the effect of an event which is irremediable absent; at the same time it is of the order of a sign to be interpreted by human beings. We might, for example, recall certain cosmic effects (meteorites) and their effects on the evolution of mammals. We immediately understand that history does not take place solely between human beings but that it has been and continues to be affected by natural events, the most decisive of which go back before the dawn of time. So the trace is the 'place' of this effect on human life, lending itself to mathematical and scientific analyses while raising our question of meaning. That is the basic reason why the form of the narrative cannot be limited to human history, but necessarily remains in the description of the evolution of life. The duality of computer discourse and narrative discourse cannot in fact be overcome, because the existence of the sciences always presupposes the basic fact that we and our historic destiny are affected by the history of nature and life, a fact which can only be narrated.

But how is it possible to safeguard in this articulation the critical element which makes it possible to prevent scientific discourse about life from surreptitiously transforming itself into myth? Paul Ricoeur distinguishes two temporal dimensions in every narrative: the 'episodic dimension' which 'draws narrative time from the side of the linear representation' and the 'configuring dimension' which transforms the succession of events, starting from 'the final point', into a signifying totality which makes it possible to 'read the end in the beginning and the beginning in the end'. Here we rediscover, at the level of discourse, what was said earlier about the 'hermeneutical circle' between the different approaches involved in the giving of meaning. The discourse on meaning is of the order of 'configuration': beginning from a continent starting point – the singular position of the person involved in it – it unfolds a significant totality. Certainly I can decide not to give meaning to my existence, or limit myself to linking events in life and history, contenting myself with these fragments of meaning without ever pronouncing on their global orientation. But if I want to give meaning to human life in the universe, I am obliged to pronounce on the whole of reality, at the same time involving the whole of my existence. Here the genre of mythical narrative is touched on and at the same time avoided. It is the specific function of the second rule to avoid this confusion. On the one hand, involvement in meaning is always a risky anticipation because the 'final point' – the starting point for any signifying configuration – is not at anyone's disposal; the meaning given is thus of the order of a postulate (to use Kant's term), capable of structuring a human existence. On the other hand, the rule of meaning forbids us to confuse the two temporal dimensions of the narrative, to use for example the episodic dimension of the history of the universe and the geo- and biospheres to construct a conclusive argument in favour of one position of meaning.

So to avoid mythical discourse is to show freedom over the question of meaning, putting one's finger on the points where the narratives of evolution risk concealing alternatives. It is on this essential point that it is necessary to do the great work of Gregory of Nyssa and a whole tradition all over again. Putting ourselves in the framework of the model of critical articulation which has just been traced here, we shall therefore now take the Christian way of giving meaning to the experience and the concept of 'life'.

II. 'The water that I shall give him will become in him a spring of water welling up to eternal life' (John 4.14)

The finitude and uniqueness of life

The distinctive point of the biblical tradition by comparison with other traditions (Hindu and Buddhist, for example) is its insistence on the uniqueness of life, which implies a certain comprehension of finitude and death. As biological beings, we are in fact totally integrated into the evolution of living beings. Death, in the strict sense of the term, appears in it with 'sexuality' (as long as beings reproduce themselves by fission or granulation there is really no such thing as death): the generation of living beings continues; death is the condition for that. Now what characterizes human beings is that they *know* that they are mortal, even if they only know it from others or by anticipation (certain drawings in prehistoric caves are eloquent testimony to this). *Our consciousness is so to speak a double one*: on the one hand we know that we are other than, more than, biological life, because we are aware of our morality (and it is the place where our desire emerges which makes us beings of flesh); and on the other hand, we also know that life would lose all its weight if we could begin it again indefinitely, constantly setting the counter back to zero. I, the example who exist, am unique; birth and death are as it were the seal put on this example, giving it – together – this unique weight which, when it suddenly rises to the surface of our consciousness, communicates to us the paradoxical experience of life a maturing within the very heart of the trials of degradation. If the first aspect of the mortality of individuals (some speak of 'avatars'), as soon as it becomes conscious, motivates the emergence of the *word* 'God' and its equivalents to express it, the other aspect, the experience of the maturing of our uniqueness, is perceived by the biblical tradition as a 'trace' of a creation or as a gift.

However, we cannot deny the profound ambivalence of this basic experience of life. Instead of being felt as a gift, the awareness of finitude and the call to accept one's own uniqueness are often the places where there is, rather, manifestation of the 'fear of being' among people, provoking their jealousy, not to say their violence. This 'infernal' link is a theme which has many variations in the biblical tradition. We want to compare our lives, which presupposes a common 'measure'. Whereas this comparison should lead us to the incomparable 'beyond measure' which is the uniqueness of each individual, it constantly slips towards jealousy and ends in the violence which seizes the life of others for its own benefit. Certainly this is an obscure process in which the uniqueness of the one can provoke, without knowing it, the jealousy of the other, and the fear of being leads to a violence which rages against the unique one standing alongside. At the root of this terrible confusion we find what scripture denounces as the lie: the suggestion, the continual insinuation, of a connivance between the limits of life – death – and a fundamental jealousy in the living world, its basic selfishness towards those who are its beneficiaries and its bearers.

Given this confusion, we can understand that according to the scriptures it is not enough to relate the origin of life; that it is also necessary to engage in a discernment or an estimation which ends up in the 'postulation' of a meaning, an act of faith about life. All these biblical attempts at evaluation finally meet up in the letter to the Romans, in particular chapter 8: 'I in fact think that the sufferings of this present time are not worth comparing with the glory that is to be revealed in us' (Rom. 8.18). The question of suffering – the question of a theodicy that has no solution is here introduced in a kind of weighing process. To weigh up is to compare the qualitative weight of things, experiences. That is the work of a whole lifetime, more particularly so when it is confronted with 'thresholds' to cross, whether these be happy or in the order of trials. This process ends up in the discovery of something 'measureless', 'beyond measure', as I already suggested earlier: a discovery of the incomparable in life which has its times and requires time. The sufferings of life have to be interpreted, the lie has to be detected; the interpretation is accompanied with groaning, and is not the capacity to groan already the sign of a transcending? In the groaning in fact a solidarity is established with the whole of the living world; however, only the compassion of the spirit of God which groans in us can take the weight and prove credible to us. This prepares for the amazing inversion of perspective when the heart and mind suddenly – in verse 28 – adopt the assessment of life by God himself, communicated in the simply proverb: 'all things work together for the good of those who love God'.

What significance is to be attached to the programme and the law?

To some degree I have just anticipated the end of our journey. In the letter to the Romans, as in other biblical texts, it goes through a decisive crossroads where the critical articulation of biology and theology also come into play. Life presupposes a separation, a structuration, the implementation of programmes, the establishment of rules of the game or the institution of a law. This protects human beings against the chaos of confusion and violence; it is like a house which is both cosmic and historical, which surrounds human life, providing it with markers.

Here there is an analogy the heuristic force of which can pose questions to theologians and researchers. As researchers are now being led to distinguish more clearly in the analysis of the human genome between the classical metaphor, DNA as *programme*, and another metaphor, DNA as *data*, so biblical scholars and theologians are more sensitive to the difference between the law and the contingent act of living, between respect for a common structure and historical access to human beings in their uniqueness, which relates to the career of all individuals in relation to others and the whole of their milieus. The term analogy maintains the differences of scale and perspective and, in particular, the emergence of human freedom. The programme and, at all events, the law are always signs of something unfinished, of a possibility which only the individual (the avatar?) can realize. In this sense they function as factors of permanence (at the level of the programme of reduplication or reproduction), or as protection (at the historical level) when jealousy and violence manifest themselves as a sign of the fear of being but also and simultaneously as promises of an increasing profusion of singularities.

Here we see a decisive bifurcation which we rediscover throughout the scriptures of the Old and New Testaments: every programme, every structure or law and its defenders, can identify themselves with 'life' and thus annul the promise given in the profusion of variations, finally doing away with the free access, autonomous and without guarantee, of subjects to their own uniqueness. The law and those who observe it can thus contribute to dissipating this lie and designating the 'source of life' which is both within and beyond the programme, the rule and the structure.

The 'source of life'

Without denying the profound continuities between the three levels of the inanimate, the animate (animal life in particular) and human life – the theory of evolution makes a powerful contribution to bringing out these continuities – with the biblical tradition we can thus can mark out thresholds and indicate characteristics: the idea of structure, programme or rule must be attributed to the inanimate world; with life, in particular the animal world, sexuality emerges as a mode of reproduction but also as a variation or idferation and all at once as a relational game – to the people of the Bible the animal world offers a model of violence (and human violence), but also the 'political' utopia of a final pacification (Isa. 11.6–9 and 65.25) in the conduct of a pacified and peaceful shepherd; and finally with the human world – men and women – there arises the possibility of uniqueness in relation, a place of desire, of surprise and an always unexpected maturing.

To suppose with the scriptures that this uniqueness in an interactive relationship is not only an 'avatar' which transmits genetic information; to postulate, in other words, that the history of the human genome cannot be reduced to the destiny of DNA as programme is already to engage in relation to the meaning of life and to lay down conditions for possibly understanding it as the 'trace' of a gift. Here the biblical tradition speaks in terms of the 'messianic openness' in its creation narratives. To interpret with the aid of this scheme the individual and phylogenetic process of the emergence and maturation of multiple forms of uniqueness in relationship does not remove any of their autonomy, since the specific nature of the free gift is precisely the withdrawal of the donor. The one who postulates the free gift of life for each and all in a unique way must, however, confront the everyday madness inflicted on this strictly 'utopian' perspective and adopt a standpoint towards the 'sufferings of the present time' (Rom. 8.18). The significance of the 'messianic openness' of the evolution of living beings is made specific here: it does not in any way relate to the concept of purpose, which has rightly been criticized by the theorists of evolution since the nineteenth century but manifests itself at the moment when the experience of the free gift of life suddenly makes people become jealous and violent and life and arouses in them the mysterious capacity to transform the life received into the gift of one's own life. The history of humankind is full of innumerable examples of this basic posture, to which the biblical tradition gives the name 'holiness' or 'sanctification of life' and which is a definitive character of the figure of the messiah.

This sanctification of life has its source in life itself; an affirmation which those feel forced to make who take seriously the idea of creation as gift. It also needs to be shown that the source of this possible sanctification goes back within human life and is rooted in the evolution of the living being, who is not reduced to structures of reciprocity but primarily manifests a generous profusion. But the biblical tradition also attributes holiness, indeed primarily and above all, to the giver of life (*zoopoios*) who effaces himself for the benefit of his gift, while bearing it and supporting it with patience. That is how we are to understand with the epistle to the Romans the mysterious relationship between the 'groanings' of the Spirit within a creation in the messianic bringing forth of holiness, and the holy God himself.

So only a trinitarian theology of 'life' of the kind suggested by the creed of 381 allows us to respect to the end the autonomy of the biological approach to evolution and at the same time to see in it the 'traces' of a messianic openness, *postulated* by believers because, without denying the elementary mechanisms of reproduction, they do not see there only the effects of a need for survival but also, and above, all the emergence, despite death, of a capacity to put at risk the uniqueness of their own lives for the benefit of the lives of others. This can only be a *postulate without guarantee*, since every other form of theological interpretation is in formal contradiction with what is postulated: a meaning of life which is fulfilled by the risky gift of the self. So the last affirmation in the creed, about the 'life of the world to come', is qualified, quite correctly, as 'expectation'. However, it would also be in contradiction with the perspective of gift to want to introduce here *in extremis* an exteriority between earthly life and eternal life which would finally take us away from the 'model of critical articulation' between the sciences and theology. *Given once for all, the gift of life is in effect – as a gift – without repentance;* so it is *in one and the same act* that believers receive their life within the world as a unique gift (creation) which they grasp for the benefit of the uniqueness of others (holiness) and that discover there the work of the Giver himself who is thus their own future (eschatology). Only this immanence of the Giver of life, which is always to come, always imminent, within the living being 'as a spring welling up to eternal life' can in fact convince believers that their estimation of the weight of life is well founded.

III. Elements of a 'spirituality' of life

These epistemological comments on the relationship between the sciences and faith and the theological reflections on the concept of life have shown that the reconstruction of evolution (in whatever form) cannot be completely abstracted from researchers themselves, their need for coherence and their desire to give meaning to their own existence in the universe. Every 'representation' of life in fact relates to those who have produced it and those who recognize themselves in it. Taking a place within this more global framework, Christian theologians can introduce here the figure of Jesus of Nazareth, confessed in the Pauline literature and in the Gospels as 'Messiah' (Mark 1.1; 8.29) and as 'the holy one of God' (John 6.69), who gives to those whom he meets on his way 'the water which becomes in the one who drinks it a source welling up to eternal life' (John 4.14). The starting point of a 'spirituality' of life is not to be found alongside our representations but in this interplay of communication between the living one who is the 'holy one of God' and those whom he engenders to the same existence. So in conclusion I want to emphasize three basic aspects of this work of engendering life which characterizes both Jesus and those who inspire his action.

The very first activity of Jesus is that of *healing* or *restoring life*. So he shows himself first and foremost sensitive to whatever threatens to bar access to the sources of life: 'every sickness and every disease among the people' (Matt. 4.23). He performs actions and says words which arouse in those whom he meets forces of self-cure, what one might call an energy of life (*dynamis*): in any case what he calls 'faith', a gift, one might say, an energy of life – 'your faith has saved you', he says to one who has just crossed the threshold of life (cf. Mark 5.21–43). It is because Jesus himself has intimate experience of the source of life in himself and because he is convinced that the act of faith which opens this source is a gift given to all that he first of all goes to those who find it difficult to get to: the disadvantaged, the sick, the outcast and the poor. So many practices indeed so many professions have formed around the healing of life. It matters little whether or not they refer explicitly to the gospel tradition. With all those who work in the service of the health of others, those who are inspired by the practice of Jesus are led to the same respect for the proper rules of this 'secularized' knowledge – the *gift* of life requires a maximum of competence – but they also discover the secret force of their own vulnerability: if they allow themselves to be touched by the patient they allow the patient to have access to their own energies of healing.

If only some benefit from the healings of Jesus, his *parables are addressed to all*, gestures in words destined, like the staff with which Moses struck the rock (Ex. 17.6), to open to those who have ears to hear sources of life 'things hidden since the foundation of the world' (Matt. 13.34). Contemporary exegesis has made us sensitive to the specific force of these little metaphorical narratives, capable of indicating within human life unprecedented possibilities which without these words would remain unseen. Their cultural roots, or rather their ways of relating themselves to life, are of little importance – some refer to the most elementary evidence of existence (e.g. Luke 7.41–43), others produce shocks by an interplay of dissonances (e.g. Matt. 20.1–16), and yet others appeal to our experience of growth (Mark 4.3–9) – all these parabolic narratives offer those to whom they are addressed a 'crossing' (Mark 4.35): put off course and oppressed by the limits of life, their senses (sight, hearing, etc) must be converted by being able to see the future. The genius of Jesus does not consists only in the fact that he found these words which open up the secret of life; it is that he spoke them in such a way that others in turn could risk their own words and invent other parables. The New Testament is the trace of this parabolic creativity; in giving us a certain 'rule' of composition (e.g. Mark 4.1–34) he invites the reader to engage in a poetic work capable of performing the function of openness to the parables of Jesus in other cultures.

Having offered some a cure and all the discovery of things hidden since the foundation of the world, Jesus initiates both into the experience of the holiness of life, into the love of enemy which characterizes the saints and makes them universally recognizable figures of life. Thus the Gospel of Matthew bases itself on the free nature of life given to all without distinction of person: 'the heavenly Father makes his sun rise on the wicked and the good and the rain fall on the just and the unjust' (Matt. 5.34–48) to reveal simultaneously the mystery of a Father God and to provide a basis for the ethical attitude which consists in becoming 'like him' and loving freely. The discovery of the free nature of the life and the invitation to give freely, even to the enemy, are by no means reserved to the disciples of Jesus: they are accessible to every human being. Matthew emphasizes this in his own way by showing the Father 'withdrawn' in 'secret' (Matt. 6.4, 6 and 18) to allow free play to the end of human gestures in favour of others. Only those who make them effectively (Matt. 25.31–46) can then perceive in the secret not a 'retreat' but the one who thus guarantees their human freedom, the Father who *gives* them to be as they are.

A 'spirituality' of life must allow itself to be informed today by this triple activity of Jesus of Nazareth. To be inspired by his practice is at the same time to note the challenge of our own creativity: it is only on this condition that the 'messiah' is truly the one who has engendered us to ourselves and whom the Spirit of the Father, thus communicated by him, proves to be the 'giver of life' (*zōopoios*). To postulate that life has a meaning thus requires Christians to adopt a style of life, a way of putting themselves every day in a globalized and pluralized world so as to be able to think correctly about the representations of life and in particular to take up a position of the theory of evolution. How can the religious traditions or other human traditions be affected by the question of the *future of life* on a globe which from now on they must look after together? The different theologies of the religions, of liberation, of the ecological preservation of life try to answer this question. They cannot alter the association between life and holiness: according to the Christian tradition it is the saints who assure a future to life, freely entrusted to each and all in a unique way. So the Christian tradition carries this future; however, it does so on condition that it leaves room for many manifestations – each time unique – of a holiness at work in all traditions and every way of giving meaning to the emergence and future of life on our globe.

Translated by John Bowden

III. The Dialogue with Faith and Theology

Evolution and Anthropology. Human Beings as the 'Image of God'

BERNARD MICHOLLET

Much water has flowed under the bridges since the nineteenth century, which saw the Catholic Church reject any idea of evolution. Even if Darwin's theory was the main object of its attacks, the prior theory of Lamarck was hardly more appreciated.[1] Today the church recognizes the autonomy of researchers in the scientific field to choose the theory which best illuminates the phenomenon of evolution.[2] So the times of the vassalage of the sciences to religion are behind us. A first explanation of this change of position is to be found in the exegetical research of first Protestants and then Catholics, which have illuminated the status of the texts. A second is beyond question connected with the attempt at reconciliation made by Teilhard de Chardin.[3] With great boldness he integrated an interpretation of facts from palaeontology into a cosmic vision of the history of humanity which cannot be too quickly dismissed, even if it is now dated.

There were numerous enthusiastic reactions to the ideas of Teilhard de Chardin. But scientists have pointed out that his finalist interpretation went beyond what the theories could bring out. And numerous theologians have noted that his conception does not adequately take account of the evil and suffering at the heart of humankind. Then the difficulties of reconciliation have been evaded by an epistemological ploy: since the domains are of two different orders, relating one to another can only lead to contradictions. To this comment the theologians have added a question: is it relevant to waste energy in elaborating such a vision, given the rapid development of knowledge?

First of all, epistemological clarification is necessary. And it should be the rule in every attempt to take account of scientific facts in theological discourse. In a culture which is sceptical about the relevance of the 'grand narratives', the difficulties noted in Teilhard de Chardin's attempt make theologians more modest. They are also mistrustful – and with reason – about anything that could resemble concordism. However, a residual question still needs to be asked: while distinguishing the orders of discourse, is it not necessary nevertheless to articulate them? The issue here is the inculturation of theological discourse in societies stamped by scientific knowledge.

I shall adopt a course which does not fail to give some account of the sciences but which does not attempt to integrate them by a 'grand narrative', aiming at a critical reception of scientific facts about evolution in a theological reflection and an evaluation of their impact on the theology of creation.

The concept of being human is bound up with the emergence of a higher order of consciousness. But by definition this consciousness cannot be perceived directly. It can only be postulated from traces which palaeontologists attempt to interpret. I shall consider the discoveries of recent decades about two hinges in the process of evolution, the transition from *Australopithecus* to *Homo habilis* and the links between *Homo neanderthalensis* and *Homo sapiens*. Then I shall raise some questions which I shall measure by two opposing theories about consciousness. I shall also allow researchers who leave only an increasingly reduced place to human beings to have their say. Finally I shall evaluate some effects of these discoveries on theological modelling: how do we interpret today the unique place of human beings created in the image of God, and depending on a continuum of life?

I. Has *Homo habilis* been deprived of his tool?

The appearance of the tool makes it possible to define a hominoid ancestor of human beings, *Homo habilis*. Now the end of the twentieth century has seen more and more discoveries which make this classification increasingly tricky. The invention of the tool itself causes difficulties.[4] In fact the remote ancestor of human beings, *Australopithecus* (dated to between four and two million years ago), is a hominid who is reputed not to have made tools. But campaigns of excavations east of Lake Turkana in Kenya have unearthed a site for making tools going back to 2.34 million years ago. There would be nothing exceptional about this did not this stratum indicate that the hominids in question were not hominoids. The researchers conclude from this that *Australopitheci* were already cutting stone before *Homo habilis*. They have thus been led to redefine the species *Homo habilis*.

This relates to the question of intelligence and consciousness. The complex cutting of tools demands a very long period of apprenticeship. The concept of a project cannot be completely absent from a being capable of such a complex activity. Now if *Homo habilis* is regarded as a hominoid, *Australopithecus* is only a hominid. Does the making of tools require being human? That is the question which is beginning to arise. Does this making of tools relate to conscious work? And in that case, what are we to think of chimpanzees who use tools, something which also requires a long apprenticeship on their part and teaching by adults? So nothing is resolved. What is clear today is that new species of *Australopithecus* have been brought to light and that the tool appeared much earlier in one of the species. The frontier between the genres *Australopithecus* and *Homo* is becoming increasingly porous.

Whatever answers are to be given to these questions, they reveal that the animal–human continuum is to be taken increasingly seriously. Do we have to see in this making of tools only a particular adaptation, analogous, for example, to birds making nests? Or are degrees of intelligence and significant consciousness already present in certain types of *Australopitheci*? On the other hand, it would seem that the complexity of research hypotheses needed to shed light on the question has been underestimated. The proliferation of ancestors is impressive. In asking ourselves about their human qualifications we are led to integrate the richness of this evolution which leads to the human being into a theological reflection.

II. A plural origin for humankind?

I consider that *Homo habilis* is at least a sufficiently distinct version of *Australopithecus* to inaugurate the genus *Homo* around 2.6 million years ago.[5] His successor is *Homo erectus*, who appeared around two million years ago. He is clearly closer to modern man. And according to various theories his posture allowed him to spread all over the surface of the earth. But what rule this diffusion played in the appearance of modern man remains a matter of discussion.[6] On the other hand, the category *Homo erectus* has become excessively wide: 'we do not truly know when *Homo erectus* begins or when he ends . . .'[7] Researchers no longer know what classification to adopt for the different specimens: are they variants of the same species or true subspecies?

This question recurs, since around 400,000 years after *Homo erectus*, *Homo sapiens* appears. Up to around 100,000 years ago the identification is made of an archaic *Homo sapiens* who has evolved closely from a *Homo erectus.*[8] The transition seems to take place very gently. To this archaic branch is attached *Homo neanderthalensis,* which appeared around 100,000 years ago, at about the same time as *Homo sapiens sapiens,* modern man. But a question immediately arises: given his characteristics, does *Homo neanderthalensis* constitute a particular species or is he a sub-species of *Homo sapiens*?[10] He has been kept apart from the species *sapiens* for more than a century. But a study of his characteristics has led researchers to put him close to *Homo sapiens sapiens.* It is in this context of increasing proximity that analyses of DNA fragments of *Homo neanderthalensis* in 1997 have shown the great distance which separates him from *Homo sapiens sapiens*. Research put his origin on the trunk of *Homo erectus* at about 500,000 years ago. This element, added to other discoveries already made, leads them to conclude clearly in favour of a species *Homo neanderthalensis*. Hence he is the cousin of *Homo sapiens sapiens.*[11]

But it must be noted that if he disappeared around 30,000 years, after cohabiting with his cousin for around 50,000 years,[12] he nevertheless had strong human characteristics. His capacities for industry were real and he had a social life, even if questions remain about his linguistic capabilities.[13] It has been established that he buried the dead.[14] So questions remain about the development of the superior functions which were the pride of his cousin. The burial of the dead is tricky to interpret. But its value must not be underestimated.

So we discover an unexpected complexity on the way that leads us to modern man. What status are we to give to *Homo neanderthalensis* in relation to *Homo sapiens sapiens*? The question of a plural origin of humanity arises, since *Homo neanderthalensis* is not an animal. Nor is he a hybrid like *Australopithecu*s. On the other hand, the problem of the genetic mixture between *Homo neanderthalensis* and *Homo sapiens sapiens* has not been resolved.

III. The emergence of consciousness

These discoveries show what an extremely complex phenomenon the appearance of consciousness is. Researchers readily attribute degrees of consciousness to animals by virtue of their situation on the scale of organic complexity.[15] They attribute a self-consciousness to certain monkeys.[16] With human beings, consciousness is thought of in relation to their linguistic capacity. It becomes uniquely refined. The leap in evolution which it implies is interpreted in very different ways. Its slow emergence in relation to the appearance of hominids and then the genus *Homo* is clear. Nevertheless, this continuity is not without apparent breaks, since different species of hominids are identified. At present there is no convincing explanation of these breaks.[17]

Sir John Eccles thinks that no scientific theory will be able to account for all this. He therefore suggests making an epistemological leap.[18] Subjective experience forces him 'to attribute the uniqueness of the self (or the soul) to a spiritual creation of a higher order'. And he dares openly to use theological language: 'Every soul is a new divine creation, implanted in the foetus at a moment between conception and birth', thus taking up a mediaeval thesis. This dualistic position is respectable. Nevertheless it risks confusing the scientific explanation of the phenomenon with its metaphysical interpretation. Without prejudging in any way the capacities of scientific explanation, it is important to engage in metaphysical reflection on the whole process of evolution so as to avoid the effect of an external and untimely divine intervention.

At the other extreme, the materialistic conception of the emergence of consciousness describes this as a product of evolution. Human consciousness 'must have arisen from former phenomena which were not in themselves conscious'.[19] Thus according to Daniel Dennett, who collects the contemporary scientific facts and tries to formalize them in materialistic thought, there is no longer any mystery. He claims that the appearance of consciousness can be explained by the notion of the pressure of selection taken from Neo-Darwinism. As the result of a chance development of their brains, new living beings benefitted from a superiority which exerted a selective pressure on the whole group. In a way the struggle for life becomes a struggle of brains. This is the course that Dennett follows to explain the place gained by brains by virtue of their growing flexibility. Furthermore, he extends his thesis by means of that of the cultural Darwinism developed by Dawkins: human beings are said to be the supports of cultural *memes* – units of cultural transmission – after being the supports of selfish genes struggling for their survival.[20]

Dennett's thesis, attractive though it is, deserves critical examination. First of all he identifies brain with consciousness. And he generalizes, as a holistic explanation of the appearance and evolution of consciousness, explanatory elements which apply to lower levels. The detailed explanations of neuronal selection at the birth of individuals[21] are associated with the notion of genetic selection, which is still by no means clear. Generalizations from theory to culture raise even more questions. Perhaps the most surprising thing is that Dennett, who is quite determined to give a scientific explanation of the emergence of consciousness, finally abandons the scientific field. Scientific method is first of all based on the analysis of a constructed object with reference to a real resistant. Thus its results have gaps. Generalizing theories primarily serve to further a deeper investigation. It is always a tricky business to make them perform a hermeneutical role, but it seems that Dennett makes them perform this role in order to establish his material conception of consciousness. He fills the scientific gaps too easily so as finally to produce the 'grand narrative' of the emergence of consciousness. This facility which he allows himself loads the various elements of scientific knowledge about the phenomenon of the development of the brain with a misunderstanding which is detrimental to research. For while it is clear that scientific research is methodologically materialistic, that does not allow conclusions to be drawn to a materialistic ontology.

It emerges from this approach is that knowledge of the evolution of the brain remains largely in the realm of hypothesis. The emergence of consciousness is far from clear. Both philosophers and theologians will remain cautious about the way in which they could exploit these modest results. But they will need to remember not to minimize too quickly the close relationships which have been brought out between cerebral capacities and consciousness.

IV. Humankind the summit of creation?

However, thanks to a theory of progress which makes human beings the culminating point of evolution,[22] human beings have not finished with those who would like to tear them from their pedestal. Lost in the universe, they have not taken well to their insertion into the continuum of life. Through Freud they have experienced a new dispossession. They are not the uncontested masters of the universe, nor even their own persons. Already in the nineteenth century a cerebral unconsciousness was discovered by researchers[23] even before the unconsciousness of psychoanalysis. This has been the object of numerous researches in neurobiology.[24] This cognitive unconsciousness, approached in an analytical way, is essential to life – and to survival! The motor zone of the brain is very often used without the regions activated by a conscious action being involved. Consciousness of an action comes about after the action has been performed.[25] In reality the functioning of the brain is far more complex than introspection might suggest to us. This is the indubitable contribution of the neuro-sciences. 'Cerebral work' on the superior functions constantly goes on without our knowing it.

Does that make human consciousness secondary? Researchers have been happy to accept the theses of Stephen Jay Gould. He has made several attacks on the idea of progress in evolution.[26] He shows that Darwin was careful not to identify the idea of evolution with that of progress. The principle of natural selection does not imply the principle of progress. The appearance of species has a contingent character which does not spare the appearance of human beings. Gould – with a secret desire to provoke? – proposes a reading based on the criterion of biomass. On this criterion, the great victors in the process of evolution are the bacteria. Evolution is not directional: 'We are the glorious accidents of an unpredictable process which shows no tendency to a greater complexity.'

That the process is strikingly unpredictable seems to be corroborated by research. But the evaluation of the tendency to complexity requires adequate criteria. Now Gould argues that there is no objective basis for describing a living organism as complex. Then he pursues his criticism of the notion of the increasing complexity in the course of evolution, basing himself on a statistical criterion and a principle of simplicity. In so doing he certainly puts into perspective the appearance of human beings within the universe. But he does not take account in a satisfying way of the fact that 'complex living beings' have not only subsisted but also developed, even if their biomass is not impressive. We are a long way from Teilhard de Chardin's law of complexity–consciousness. But are a statistical criterion and a principle of simplicity enough to provide an interpretation of the phenomenon of evolution? Elevated to the rank of hermeneutical principles, they come into competition with other principles from other sciences used in the study of human beings within the context of life. Gould's reflection finally draws attention to the 'hypertrophy of the ego of humanity within the universe'.

V. The 'creation of humankind by God'

What place remains for the interpretation of the emergence of humankind as God's creation? The 'grand narratives' which re-enchant our cold world are disqualified. The spiritualist narratives are suspected of exceeding the authorized interpretation of the scientific facts which can be obtained without appealing to God. And the material narratives do not long withstand a careful analysis of the process of interpretation that they employ. They slide too easily from the methodological materialism of the sciences to the adoption of a materialistic philosophical position, without respecting a critical epistemological authority. Finally, current fragmentary knowledge resists all easy attempts to offer a narrative perspective.

Another effect of these researches is to prompt a healthy reticence in the philosopher which prevents too rapid a development of a philosophy of nature. Contemporary attempts based on some postulates display native frailties. In fact, new knowledge often destroys the coherence that is emphasized. It clashes with a knowledge which is both incomplete and too great. It lowers its guard when faced with islands of unexpected and resistant complexity.

In these conditions, theological research will use concepts relating to a philosophy of nature as a philosophical intermediary without envisaging its holistic character. Contemporary research and questions call on the theology of creation to note the following:

1. The animal–human continuum is very strong (human characteristics preceded modern man).
2. Does humankind have only the form that we know today?
3. The development of consciousness is an evolutionary process which culminates in human beings but goes beyond them.
4. A phenomenon of socio-cultural evolution takes over from the process of biological evolution.
5. Humankind remains a fragile species in the midst of others, even if it seems to have been successful.

1. *The animal–human continuum* has already prompted numerous pieces of research in the wake of Teilhard de Chardin. Today it seems to be more and more pronounced and more and more complex. In the end we must note the chance nature of the emergence of human beings in a theology of creation. Theories which regard creation as a divine game have been put forward to express that. They would seem weak in relation to the segments of intelligence present in the universe which the sciences have succeeded in unveiling.[27] They certainly convey the novelty of creation, but hide a quest for the significance of the emergence of consciousness. The sciences show how vast is the autonomy of the development of the created. They come to be in tension with Genesis 1–2, which emphasizes the separation between human beings created in the image of God and other living beings. They can then base themselves on the theological work about the divine discretion which presides over the deployment of the universe.

2. *To evoke several forms of humanity* to take account of *Homo neanderthalensis* is to ask for trouble. Relevant neither to theological fiction nor to anthropological ignorance, isn't this a theoretical question which is of no use for our salvation? That is probably the case if we judge that human beings are once and for all imprisoned in a definition which does not shock aesthetics. However, our humankind is made up of men and women who do not correspond to the canons of a healthy anthropology of the subject. They bear genetic, cerebral or psychological defects which irremediably affect their higher functions. Some of their like are at times afraid to see them as brothers and sisters. But who will dare to say that these are not human? We have put them in the category of exceptions to which we do not refer, above all so as not to disturb our thinking, which rebels against the harshness of reality. In that case we will consider the question of the humanity of *Homo neanderthalensis* as a limit question aimed at keeping our eyes open to real humanity. The human being created in Genesis 1–2 is not described in accordance with the canons of a perfect, finished anthropology. How can real humanity with plural origins bear the concept of the image of God?

3. *The development of consciousness* is certainly the guideline for reflection on the emergence of humankind. However, animals are not devoid of a certain consciousness, and human beings who are conscious of themselves largely remain an unknown factor to themselves. They are no longer their own masters. Here we come up against the difficulty of thinking of the privilege which humanity has of hearing the call of God. Even if human capacities can be taken as indications which allow us to think that human beings have a 'spiritual soul',[28] they remain insufficient. And finally, as a first stage, the impact of the sciences on theology will be to send theology back to an anthropological analysis of the religious, spiritual and philosophical traditions of humanity. As a second stage, in an acceptance of the word of God in Jesus Christ, theology can affirm that it discerns in human beings a 'transcendental openness', to use Rahner's term. As far as humanity is concerned, the creative call to life is that which opens it to its creator in accordance with a mode which radically transcends the creative call to the universe as a whole. So we can say that the creation of humankind resides in this call. That gives it its origin by finalizing it. From now on, to be human will be more a duty than a state.

4. *A phenomenon of socio-cultural evolution* which extends biological evolution is at work within humanity. Often put in question because of the dramas experienced by humankind, it was over-emphasized by Teilhard de Chardin. It was his Achilles' heel. However, without forgetting the crimes of

the twentieth century in particular, it is by no means certain that we must abandon this reflection, since it is deeply rooted in the everyday life of men and women. The improvement of our living conditions and our cultural level have a marked effect on the development of human capacities. Contemporary research into the flexibility of the human brain shows how it is the product of a genetic determination and an interaction with the environment. A baby's brain emerges as a product marked indelibly by its environment. This fact requires society to assume its responsibilities in the process of human development. While God may be the creator, we need to open our eyes to 'the human beings which fashion their own humanity'.[29] This focusses our attention on the advent of human subjects through human relationships formed by the man–woman relationship.

5. *Humankind remains a fragile species* inserted into nature in the midst of other species. Our greatness does not reside in our capacity to bring the rest of creation to its knees. The greatness of humankind in the face of the bacteria does not reside in its biomass, as Pascal well perceived in meditating on the 'thinking dew'. To think of the image of God emerging from a nature with which it has a vital connection is the beginning of the theological theses which make nature as a whole the creature in the image of God. In that case, the status of human beings is primarily that of the beings which owe their existence to nature.[30] Following the awareness of their insertion into nature in a continuum of life, human beings want to fuse with this creation. Here they are responding to the ecological concern and are taking serious account of their status as a species, which owes its existence to nature. Nevertheless, is the 'mediating character of nature in the work of creation' sufficient for Gilkey to foist on it the attributes traditionally reserved to human beings? And is there not a risk of the idolatry of nature, which would come to oppose a true liberation of human beings called on to act in a responsible way?

VI. The image of God

Finally, the theological issues emerging from current research are of three orders. The creation of humankind by God does not make humankind a non-natural object, far less an anti-natural one. Does the continuum of life and the insertion of humankind within animal species authorize the levelling down of creatures within a nature decked out in attributes which are human and sometimes divine? How is the responsibility of humankind in its self-fashioning and within nature itself a dimension of the creative act?

Having done away with the 'grand narratives', must we now re-enchant theological discourse by a holistic approach which does not explain all its presuppositions? In particular, this disguises the fact that it attributes a metaphysical weight to the natural phenomena studied by the sciences. The emergence of human beings within a process can be interpreted as a divine call in a discretion which allows the advent of the subject. To seek to emphasize the vital links which unite human beings and nature is laudable, provided that this is not translated into an enslavement of human beings to supposed laws. On the contrary, to keep the character of human responsibility, it is necessary for human beings to be liberated.

For that, is it not necessary to recentre the concept of the image of God on Jesus Christ, the perfect image of God? This is no longer a matter of an 'Omega Point', finalizing creation by a quasi-deterministic recapitulation put in perspective by a 'grand narrative'. Our objective is to maintain, in accordance with two distinct ontological orders, while tying them together, the bonds woven between nature and humankind and the relations between human beings who structure this humanity. As a hypothesis I suggest that we should rethink Jesus Christ as the image of God. This is not the image which takes up the human desire to be purely and simply copied. It must be conceived as the mark on humankind of the creative call of God. This image of God as such, which is ultimately a norm, liberates humankind on its way of humanization. Humankind is called to recognize in Jesus Christ, the image of God, the figure of the future which is put in its hands. In the discretion which characterizes his action, God opens to humanity, by giving himself to it as Spirit, the free space which it needs to invent itself in relation to his image refracted in the community that bears witness at the heart of the world.

Translated by John Bowden

Notes

1. In 1860, the provincial council of Cologne declared that transformism applied to the human body is contrary to scripture.
2. Cf. the position of John Paul II in his message to the Pontifical Academy of Sciences on 22 October 1966 (*Osservatore Romano*, 24 October 1996): 'new knowledge leads us to recognize that the theory of evolution is more than a hypothesis'. I shall leave aside here the problem of North America biblical fundamentalism, which requires specific analysis (cf. Dominique Lecourt, *L'Amérique entre la Bible et Darwin*, Paris 1992).

3. The posthumous publications (especially *The Phenomenon of Man,* 1955) had been preceded by an important underground influence from his ideas. *Humani generis*, which recognizes evolution within certain limits, goes back to 1950.
4. Cf. the discoveries by Hélène Roche, *Nature*, 5 May 1999.
5. I shall follow the dominant opinion of research workers, leaving them the task of settling this new debate and making the dates of the various transitions more precise.
6. Romain Pigeaud, 'Histoires de famille chez *Homo erectus*', *La Recherche*, Paris, no. 329, June 1999.
7. Ibid., 32.
8. In reality the appearance of *Homo sapiens* remains difficult to date between -400,000 and -100,000 years.
9. Cf. Jean-Jacques Hublin, 'Climat de l'Europe et origine des Néanderthaliens', *Pour la Science*, 'Les origines de l'humanité', dossier hors-série, Paris, January 1999.
10. Cf. Claude-Louis Gallien, *Homo – Histoire plurielle d'un genre très singulier*, Paris 1998.
11. These researches are continuing: the DNA analyses require further confirmation.
12. The estimation of the duration of the cohabitation remains controversial.
13. Anatomical research shows that his linguistic capacity must have been inferior to that of *Homo sapiens sapiens.*
14. Indications in some places even suggest a 'spirituality'.
15. Cf. Derek Denton, *The Pinnacle of Life. Consciousness and Self-awareness in Humans and Animals*, St Leonard's, Australia 1993.
16. The experiments with mirrors and chimpanzees lead to this conclusion (Gallup, 1975).
17. Hopes are based on research into the mechanisms involved in the process of evolution and their genetic bases.
18. Cf. John C. Eccles, *Evolution of the Brain: Creation of the Self*, London and New York 1989.
19. Cf. Daniel C. Dennett, *Consciousness Explained*, New York 1991, Chapter 6.
20. Cf. Richard Dawkins, *The Selfish Gene,* Oxford 1976.
21. Cf. Jean-Pierre Changeux, *L'homme neuronal*, Paris 1983, and M. Edelman, *Bright Air, Brilliant Fire: On the Matter of Mind,* New York 1992. These researchers too are not completely free of a desire for hasty generalization.
22. I shall not touch on the discussions on the 'anthropic principle' here.
23. Cf. Marcel Gauchet, *L'inconscient cérébral*, Paris 1882.
24. Cf. Pierre Buser, *Cerveau de soi, cerveau de l'autre*, Paris 1998, ch.6.
25. The motor zone of the brain is activated; so this a more complex phenomenon than the reflex arc. Information circulates more rapidly in the visual zone in the

direction of the motor zone than in the direction of the zone which allows identification.

26. Stephen Jay Gould, *Full House*, New York 1996.
27. Jacques Arnould, *La théologie après Darwin*, Paris 1998, notes this fragility in the theses of Harvey Cox and Jürgen Moltmann.
28. In this case I am referring to a Thomistic terminology.
29. For a suggestive reading of Gen. 1–3 the psychoanalyst Marie Balmary shows how the advent of the subject is rooted in the man–woman relationship, a mediation responding to the call of the creator 'in his image' (cf. *La divine origine – Dieu n'a pas créé l'homme*, Paris 1993).
30. Cf. Langdon Gilkey, *Nature, Reality and the Sacred – The Nexus of Science and Religion*, Minneapolis 1993; and a recent discussion by Gregory R. Peterson, 'The Evolution of Consciousness and the Theology of Nature', *Zygon – Journal of Religion and Science* 34.2, June 1999.

Evolutionary Theory and Biblical Discourse

ANTONY F. CAMPBELL

From the outset it is important to recognize that there is no one biblical discourse on creation, just as there is no one theory of evolution. Biblical unity can be found in the affirmation that the world is created by God; evolutionary unity can be found in the affirmation that the world evolves. Both statements say a lot and, at the same time, not very much at all.

My aim in this article is to provide Bible non-specialists with access to where some Bible specialists may stand with regard to the biblical text and where major aspects of the biblical text are with regard to creation and evolution and, by implication, much of matters scientific. Occasionally it is important to grapple with the difficult issues where the Bible interfaces with science or theology.

One of the tasks of third-millennium theology will be to work out more precisely the role that scripture has in faith and theology. The popular paradigm is outmoded and in many areas abandoned. In an archaic caricature ('one verse, one vote') it is no longer respectable in either theory or practice. In more refined forms (where scripture once appropriately assessed is considered determinative), it is largely abandoned in theoretical considerations – under pressure from the biblical texts themselves – while still prevailing all too widely in practical contexts.

Biblical texts – not modern prejudices – thrust themselves on scriptural interpreters often quite insistently in an invitational role. They invite thought; they seldom impose or determine it – no matter how much we might like them to. A reciprocal movement – a mutual interaction – operates between the influence of scripture and the experience of faith. Third-millennium theology must increasingly explore this reciprocity. The roles of scripture are multiple; the experience of faith finds expression in multiple ways. The interplay between these is what gives shape to faith in any given generation.

Observation of hallowed practice suggests the proposition: people do not believe as true whatever they can quote from the Bible; they quote from the Bible what they believe to be true.[1] The question then becomes: why do people believe something to be true? People choose the image of the God they believe in. People choose the biblical texts they quote because these texts express their belief. Theology has yet to explore to the full both why people believe what they do and how it should evaluate the beliefs people choose to hold.

The plurality of biblical approaches denies the existence of a unified biblical discourse on creation. It would be unwise to assume that there is any single evolutionary discourse on the existence of our world and universe.[2] It will worry neither scientist nor theologian that evolution is a theory. Scientists, theologians and biblical specialists spend their lives in the midst of hypotheses and theories. For some, evolution is postulated along with a denial of the presence of God; for others, evolution is postulated along with a belief in the presence of God. For the latter, the evolution of God's universe may be described as unguided, or guided, or risked. 'Unguided': God created the universe and left it to its own devices – in most Christian theology, dismissed along with the eighteenth-century Deists. 'Guided': affirms God's creative activity, initial and continued, and allows for the presence in one form or another of this divine activity and of evolution, so that the universe is as God wills it to be. 'Risked': might affirm that God took the risk of creating an evolutionary universe, is with it in its evolution (with joy and sorrow, happiness and pain), but does not control it so that the universe is as evolution has brought it to be.

Much moderate Christian theology settled for 'guided', with the language of divine direction or divine supervision and perhaps the separation of evolution in the physical realm from the realm of mind and spirit. The possibility of 'risked' is still to be fully explored. Human minds may prefer a mingling of possibilities rather than a rigid separation, a mingling allowing for different metaphors at different moments; divine mystery may settle for much the same.

My own fancy is held by 'risked': I believe that Judaeo–Christian faith has long affirmed God's commitment to creation and God's presence with all that happens in creation. Is that creative act best envisaged as God's supreme risk? The risk: God created the context for the evolutionary development of our universe, a development God was present to or in, but did not guide. Such a view is attractive when we are faced by with all the horrors of our world. Rather than deal with the intellectual difficulty of a God responsible for all that we find repulsive, we accept a God who journeyed with us in our evolution, rejoicing in all that was of worth in our evolutionary trajectory – and pained by all that was not. An evolutionary world entails risks. How many of us would want God to have held back before these risks?

Evolution has been pitted against Christianity as 'a merciless survival of the fittest' opposed to the central biblical message. This is not fair to all forms of evolutionary theory – just as the granite of *laissez-faire* is not the only face of modern capitalism. The phrase 'survival of the fittest' was coined by Herbert Spencer; Darwin preferred 'natural selection'.[3] As a biologist friend remarked: evolution is about the diversification of life, about species finding niches and thriving in them. There are niches for both the wolf and the lamb.[4] Co-operation rather than competition can emerge as a leitmotif of evolutionary theory. Cultures tend to articulate new discoveries in ways that support their cultural self-understanding.

Compatibility with the Bible is still an issue. Biblical portrayals of creation evidence manifest plurality. Often the understanding of creation in biblical texts is nuanced to fit the context in which creation is evoked. Creation texts in the Bible have God involved with the world. Evolutionary theory that does not dismiss God's relationship with the world is unlikely to prove incompatible with biblically based faith.

Creationism, on the other hand, claims its authority from the Bible and sets its face firmly against evolution. By 'creationism' is meant the view that the universe and all things in it were created directly by God and are not the result of a long evolutionary process; this applies with particular force to forms of life. It is based on the account of creation in the book of Genesis, understood literally as a descriptive account, and thus has links with fundamentalism. Claiming to be, as a theory, of the same status as any other proposed (scientific) account, it emerged in the 1960s in the USA (though with roots in the nineteenth century) in direct contest with the theory of evolution associated with Charles Darwin . . .[5]

As a Bible person, it maddens me to read claims that creationism takes the Bible literally. It does not. There are numerous portrayals of creation in the Bible and there are radical differences between them. Three of the combat variety are noted by way of allusion and reference. They portray a picture of creation by combat between the God of Israel and the forces of chaos. They portray a picture of creation that should send shivers down a creationist's spine. No wonder these portrayals seldom get a mention. Two others are lengthier, more direct, and better known to us. In fact we are so familiar with them, in Genesis 1 and 2, that we often do not notice how widely they differ from each other.[6]

The Bible has at least three images of the creator God: the fighter God, the co-operator God, and the proclaimer God. Common to all three is the noun God; it is the unifying factor for creation texts. Different in each is the modifying noun – fighter, co-operator, proclaimer – that proclaims the biblical discourse's openness to whatever includes God.

Other texts have other approaches: for example, Psalm 104.5–9 or Psalm 136.4–9, or with a more lateral approach as in Proverbs 8.22–31. The nature of the creative process often may not be addressed. Israel believed in a creator God; that should be beyond doubt. Israel used its belief in creation in a variety of ways for maximum theological effect. Belief in God as creator was a resource for life and prayer – not for freezing into the formulations of dogma.

Dogma out of place is bad enough; pseudo-science is worse. I do not begrudge scientists their complaint that creationists distort, misunderstand and misapply science in the presentation of their creationist views. It is the right of scientists to defend their bailiwick. I object intensely to any claim by creationists or on behalf of creationists that their view emerges from a literal understanding of the Bible. The Bible is my bailiwick and I will defend it. Creationism as a literal understanding of the Bible is bunk.

The fighter God

Creation in Psalms 74 and 89. Psalm 74 is a community lament, with an appeal to God's creative power in the middle of it. God is a mighty fighter who deals summarily with the opposition forces:

> You divided the sea by your might:
> you broke the heads of the dragons in the waters.
> You crushed the heads of Leviathan:
> you gave him as food for the creatures of the wilderness (vv. 13–14).

Leviathan and the sea and the dragons are all figures of chaos in the mythology known to us from the ancient Near East. Under different guises or names, they will recur in the texts of Job and Isaiah. There should be no doubt of the power and universality of the creator God in Psalm 74:

> Yours is the day, yours also the night:
> you established the luminaries and the sun.
> You have fixed all the bounds of the earth:
> you made summer and winter (vv. 16–17).

Why does Israel appeal to a God of raw power in this psalm? Because 'the enemy has destroyed everything in the sanctuary' (v. 3). 'How long, O God, is the foe to scoff? Is the enemy to revile your name for ever?' (v. 10). In such circumstances, what the singer of psalms wants from God is power, raw power, the sort of power that can shatter God's foes and encourage God's friends, the power displayed in shattering the forces of chaos at creation.

Psalm 89 is in essence another community lament. It begins with a portrayal of God, 'feared in the council of the holy ones, great and awesome above all that are around him' (v. 7). So it hymns God's power in creation:

> You rule the raging of the sea;
> when its waves rise, you still them.
> You crushed Rahab like a carcass;
> you scattered your enemies with your mighty arm.
> The heavens are yours, the earth also is yours;
> the world and all that is in it – you have founded them.
> The north and the south – you created them;
> Tabor and Hermon joyously praise your name (vv. 9–12).

Here we meet the sea again and the new figure of Rahab, along with the enemies of God. At this point, the evocation of divine power does not emerge out of the powerlessness of Israel; that finds expression towards the end of the psalm. It emerges out of the psalmist's desire to find words and images to express the unique supremacy of Israel's God. Yet it is not divorced from Israel's need of God's supremacy and power.

Creation in Job 7, 9, and 26. Several times in the book Job appeals to the image of the creator God. The image is that of the raw irresistible power of the mighty fighter.

> Am I the sea or the dragon
> that you set a guard over me? (7.12).
> God will not turn back his anger:
> the helpers of Rahab bowed beneath him.
> How then can I answer him,
> choosing my words with him? (9.13–14).
> By his power he stilled the Sea;
> by his understanding he struck down Rahab.
> By his wind the heavens were made fair;
> his hand pierced the fleeing serpent.
> These are indeed by the outskirts of his ways;

and how small a whisper do we hear of him!
But the thunder of his power who can understand? (26.12–14)

In these passages, we meet the sea, the dragon (in Hebrew, Tannin), Rahab and 'the fleeing serpent' – all figures in the combat myths of creation.

Job is no stranger to the most sublime literary language of creation. See, for example, either the immediately preceding verses here (26.6–11) or the magnificent imagery of Job 31.1, in God's discourse from the whirlwind.

Why then does Job use this combat creation language and imagery? Because, in his conflict with his friends, Job paints an image of a God of irresistible and aggressive power. Job is livid with anger against this God:

What are human beings,
that you make so much of them,
that you set your mind on them,
visit them every morning,
test them every moment?
Will you not look away from me for a while,
let me alone until I swallow my spittle?
If I sin, what do I do to you, you watcher of humanity?
Why have you made me your target?
Why have I become a burden to you?
Why do you not pardon my transgression
and take away my iniquity? (7.17–21).

At this point in his journey Job feels attacked by God, and he resents it. The helpless state of the creature confronting the creator God is what Job feels and what Job would like to be freed from: 'How then can I answer him, choosing my words with him?' (9.14). Job's plea to God is: 'Withdraw your hand far from me, and do not let dread of you terrify me' (13.21).

The book of Job draws on the language of creation by combat and the image of God as mighty fighter in order to convey Job's frustration at his inability to meet God on even terms, as one prince to another (cf. 31.37).

Creation in Isaiah 27 and 51. Isaiah 51 reflects the agony of exiles who long to return home. The agony finds words in poetry that is both plea and promise.

Awake, awake, put on strength,
O arm of the LORD! Awake, as in days of old,
the generations of long ago!

Was it not you who cut Rahab in pieces,
who pierced the dragon?
Was it not you who dried up the sea,
the waters of the great deep;
who made the depths of the sea a way
for the redeemed to cross over?
So the ransomed of the LORD shall return,
and come to Zion with singing . . . (51.9–11).

Here again, we meet Rahab, the dragon (Tannin), and the sea (and the deep that was covered by darkness in Gen. 1.2). Almost like a modern film-maker, Isaiah blends the image of the sea, dried up in creation, into the image of the sea divided at the exodus. So creation blends into salvation. The power of the God who subdued Rahab and the dragon is the power at God's disposal for the salvation and return of those in exile-the return to Zion with singing.

Isaiah draws on this imagery of awesome power because of the exiles' need to have faith in a God who has the capacity to bring them home.

Elsewhere in the book of Isaiah, the prophecy points to a future time when God will restore order to creation. The passage Isaiah 24.20–27.1 begins by pointing to the future when God will punish the host of heaven' (24.20) and 'the moon will be abashed, and the sun ashamed' (24.23). The passage ends with imagery that is by now familiar:

> On that day the LORD with his cruel and great and strong sword will punish Leviathan the fleeing serpent, Leviathan the twisting serpent, and he will kill the dragon that is in the sea (27.1).

Before we moderns are too easily dismissive of primitive mythology, we need to be aware that these combat images occur in some of the most sophisticated literature of our Bible: Isaiah, Job and Psalms. The power of God is celebrated as creator, magnificently superior to the forces of chaos: the dragon, the serpent, the sea, Leviathan, Rahab, Tannin – the enemies of God. This is creation faith used for maximum theological effect.

The co-operator God

Creation in Genesis 2. Actually, the text we are looking at is Gen. 2.4b–25. 'Genesis 2' is a comfortable shorthand, and 'Genesis 1' will be a similar shorthand for Gen. 1.1–2.4a. Genesis 2 is the text of the co-operative artist, we might almost say 'artisan'. The God of Genesis 2 is a working God:

> Then the LORD God formed man from the dust of the ground . . . . (2.7).

Similarly, in pursuit of a partner for the man:

> Out of the ground the LORD God formed every animal of the field and every bird of the air, and brought them to the man to see what he would call them; and whatever the man called every living creature, that was its name (2.19).

'Every animal' and 'every bird' would have used up a lot of 'ground' and surely left a weary God. Yet it is the God of Genesis 1 who will rest on the seventh day from all the work that he had done – who hardly 'worked' at all (cf. Gen. 2.2).

A lot of people forget the major differences between this account of creation and the account in Genesis 1. In Genesis 1, of course, everything is created, including the earth and its vegetation, birds and beasts, man and woman. Yet in Genesis 2 these are created again – vegetation, birds and beasts, the man and the woman. The order is strikingly different. In Genesis 1, man and woman are created together and are created last (1.26–27). In Genesis 2, man and woman are created separately, with the man created at the beginning of the account and his incompleteness brought to partnered completion in the creation of the woman at the end of the account (cf. 2.7 and 22). Not only is the order different, but the images of the beginning are as different as night and day. Genesis 1 begins in the dark and the wet: 'darkness covered the face of the deep, while a wind from God swept over the face of the waters' (1.2). Genesis 2 begins in barren dryness, with no plant and no herb and no water, 'for the LORD God had not caused it to rain upon the earth, and there was no one to till the ground' (2.5). Notice the assumption that we humans would till the ground, long before there is any talk of sin. The initial situation is barren and dry; it is evocative of the searing light of the desert sun.

What do we make of a text like this? The co-operative labouring God is not one of the staple figures of Israelite theology. It may be that the biblical narrative is portraying Israel's (and our) distancing from intimacy with God. This is the God whose nearness allowed the first humans to hear 'the sound of the LORD God walking in the garden at the time of the evening breeze' (3.8). A story of increasing distance between creature and Creator needs to start with a creation story of intimacy and co-operation.

One caution is needed by Christians reading Genesis 2–3. Human work is taken for granted from the start (Gen. 2.5, 15). Immortality is not given to the couple (Gen. 3.22–24). The punishments formulated in the singular for the woman and the man are not applied to later generations (3.16–19). Only the instinctive antipathy of humans for snakes is specified (3.15). Anyone familiar with the ancestral and dynastic promises will be struck by the absence of any reference to future generations. Nowhere in the rest of the Hebrew scriptures is reference made to this story of disobedience (cf. Sir. 40.1 and esp. 49.16). A classical presentation of original sin is not to be found in Genesis 2–3.

The proclaimer God (who keeps sabbath)

Creation in Genesis 1. And so we come to the text so beloved of those who talk about creationism. Into the darkness of the formless void and the windswept deep, God by the sheer power of proclamation launches brilliantly symbolic light (1.3). There are many activities of God in the chapter: God sees, God separates, God calls, God makes, God commands the waters and the earth, God creates, and God blesses. Above all, God says.

This is the account of the majestic proclaimer. At every stage, there is the basic proclamation, 'And God said.' No matter how many activities God performs – separating, making, commanding, creating, blessing – the over-arching statement is always: 'And God said.' There is no question here of God forming anything from the ground. The earth is commanded to bring forth vegetation (v. 11) and living creatures of every kind (v. 24 – although in v. 25, God makes the animals). There is no question of God bringing his creation to the man and talking with him about it and its names. God created humankind in God's image and likeness. That is the closest we come in this account to intimacy. The God of Genesis 1 is a majestic and distant proclaimer.

What can never be overlooked is that all the activity of creation is fitted into six days, thanks to a couple of activities on the third and sixth days. So the seventh day is empty and God is able to hallow it as the sabbath day. It is a great pity that we have no English word to convey the identity of 'resting' and 'sabbath'. Twice our English translations note that 'God rested' on the seventh day (2.2 and 3). The Hebrew verbs *yišbōt* (2.2) and *šābat* (2.3) mean 'rested', 'ceased work'; the association with the Hebrew noun for sabbath (*šābat*) is unmistakable. They can be heard as saying: 'And God sabbathed.'

Here Israel's scriptures open with a statement that the God of all creation, the Lord of heaven and earth, the God responsible for all that we can see and touch, this God is a God who 'sabbathed on the seventh day'. And only Israel in all the earth observed sabbath. Israel might be defeated and overwhelmed by the mightier political powers of its day. But Israel encountered its God in its sabbath. Everything that Israel saw – from the light and sky to the earth and sea, the plants and trees, the sun and moon and stars, the birds and beasts – everything reminded Israel of the God who created by majestic proclamation and then sabbathed, rested on the seventh day. And only Israel in all the earth observed sabbath. It is a faith statement of the highest order.

Deuteronomy says: 'What other great nation has a God so near to it as the LORD our God is whenever we call to him?' (Deut. 4.7). Genesis 1 says: 'What other great nation has a God who has created the heavens and the earth and who sabbaths as we alone do?' In the unstable and insecure world of exile Genesis 1 stood as a faith statement affirming stability and security in the power of God.

Conclusion

It is a sad day for us when we allow ourselves to be persuaded to abandon all this theological wealth and believe that when we take the Bible literally we find so insipid a message as pseudo-science. It would be a fearful misunderstanding to believe that the Bible blocked our access to evolutionary thinking.

Notes

1. Cf. A. F. Campbell and M. A. O'Brien, *The International Bible Commentary,* Collegeville, MN 1998, 57–8.
2. Different points of view may be found, for example, in E. O. Wilson, *Consilience: The Unity of Knowledge*, New York: Knopf 1998; A. O'Hear, *Beyond Evolution*, Oxford 1997; T. Nagel, *The Last Word*, Oxford 1996, and many others.
3. See H. Hearder, *Europe in the Nineteenth Century 1830–1880*, London 1966, 343.
4. I owe this observation to John Sweeney of the Center for Theological Reflection, Mexico City.
5. From the article 'Creationism' in *The Oxford Dictionary of World Religions,* ed. John Bowker, Oxford 1997, 244.
6. What follows is a slightly adapted version of my article, 'Creationism! Utterly Unbiblical', *Eureka Street,* May 1997, 30–4. It is used with permission.

Bible and Evolution. Two Codes – Two Messages*

BAS VAN IERSEL

In December 1995, under the title 'Eat and be Eaten'. I read the review of a book by Richard Dawkins with the biblical-sounding title *River Out of Eden. A Darwinian View of Life*. Dawkins sees the river of paradise in Genesis 2 as the river of genetic information which flows from the paradise of creation, namely DNA with information and codes for building the body, which can continue and multiply. According to the author, the genes, the bearers of DNA, are selfish, since they are engaged in harsh competition for a future in which only the strongest wins. In other words, those who look at nature see only a struggle for existence to reproduce successful genes in a hostile environment. Darwin's 'fight for survival' and his 'survival of the fittest' are thus given a new and topical context, a contemporary form, but now with the challenging old conclusion in a post-Darwinian version. As a reviewer put it: 'The reason for our life, our fate, our destiny or our meaning is . . . none other than the survival of our DNA.' When a few days later I heard the message from a well-known preacher on the radio that one of the problems most neglected by the church was the theory of evolution, though this is unconsciously taken for granted by each of us, I felt all the more obliged to reflect on the matter and to formulate my thoughts.

However, the reviewer of the book also pointed out that Dawkins did not go into the handing on of non-genetic information. I began to reflect on that. I did not want primarily to oppose the theory of evolution; rather, I presuppose that there are many indications that it is correct. However, if the theory of evolution is true, it need not be the whole truth. Thus, to give an example, the verses of scripture quoted by Bloemers in his article (Koheleth 3.19–21) may indeed be right in saying that human beings and animals are subject to the same fate, for both return to the dust. But this text completely neglects its own existence. The text, which comes from a document from presumably the third century before Christ, cannot have been written by an animal, but only by one of the children of men mentioned in it. So there are also differences.

I. Brain, speech and writing

That indicates my planned approach. In the review I mentioned I read about the transition from animal to human life: 'Thus in the course of millions of years a system has come into being which uses data from sensory perception and stores them in a memory: what is meant is the brain. Finally this brain becomes conscious of itself and develops speech: *Homo sapiens* is born. This speech forms a communicative network in which brains exchange information and develop a common technology of survival.'

Of course speech presupposes the existence of several beings with brains who get into contact with one another with the help of linguistic signs and not only transfer but also exchange information. Now this transformation of information with the help of spoken speech has clear limitations. It presupposes that the users of spoken language can perceive one another and their expressions directly or indirectly, in other words that this transference can take place only when the two are simultaneously present. But in addition to this capacity for speech, human evolution has also made it possible to make use of visual signals or a written language – later, at the same time or perhaps even earlier. This began with simple marks with which one could identify for oneself or for others a very tall tree as a good look-out post over the environment, a particular cave as a safe hiding place, or a path through the wood as the fastest way to a destination. Later this development developed into a complicated system of writing alongside, and in part parallel, to spoken language. But writing makes it possible to keep signals and extended texts for a long time, indeed a very long time. The inventor of the saying *verba volant, scripta manent* (words fly away, what is written remains) already knew that anything written remains as long as the material and the written signs remain and can be reached. In that case it can be read and understood by everyone who sees the written signs and knows the codes used by the writer.

II. Only aimed at survival?

Here we can raise the question whether the cultural information is not gradually directed towards other needs than survival. For not only do speech and writing become more complicated, not only can they also serve other goals than mere survival, but also the communities in which they function organize themselves in a more comprehensive way: their members can allow themselves activities which are no longer related to survival, like the practice of art and the investigation of scientific foundations.

As a consequence of this, in the course of the century which lies behind us an immeasurable amount of cultural information of the most varied kinds and about the most varied things has been accumulated. This includes works of art like drawings, paintings and mosaics, sculpture and buildings, music scores, plays and film scripts, films and videotapes, gramophone records, tapes, compact discs, diskettes and really anything which – whether or not deliberately – can be used as a vehicle of information, even down to traffic signs, T-shirts or sports clothes. But the most important part of cultural information exists in the form of writings which are preserved as manuscripts or printed works and have been made accessible in museums, archives, libraries and documentation centres.

As I have already indicated, the special character of these writings lies in the fact that – unlike genetic information, which is transferred only in time from one generation to the next – they can hand on their information directly over many generations. Anyone who, for example, has learned cuneiform, can still read the Codex Hammurabi in the Louvre. And anyone who has not learned cuneiform can get to know it with the help of translations of the text. Of course this cultural information relates to a much shorter period than the many millennia in which genetic information has been handed on, but writing has its own form of reproduction. For the genetic information in human genes constantly changes. As the DNA in a new individual is a combination of his or her father's and mother's DNA, the genetic information constantly changes. In contrast to this, the information from writings exists and is accessible in its original form. Therefore in the Louvre we can still read the same Codex of Hammurabi that the authors and sculptors chiselled and cut in stone. And at will, those interested in many centuries can discovery in a library the writings of Descartes or current traffic regulations, provided that these are preserved for coming generations.

III. The Bible

The Bible also belongs to this reservoir of past writings, preserved in Hebrew and Greek hand-written copies and in printed texts, in virtually endless translations into most languages, and spread all over the world. The authors of the Second Testament called the books of the First Testament 'the scriptures', and thus declared them to be most important works that were written at that time. They added a number of the narratives and letters to them and together these texts form for us Christians 'scripture' or the Bible. This has various forms and is less fixed than one might expect of a canonical scripture. Granted, the Jews have their Tenach, i.e. the Hebrew version of what Christians call the First Testament, but they claim that the Tenach is incomprehensible without the oral Torah (which then in turn is set down in later documents as the Mishnah). Alongside the Hebrew Bible which has been mentioned there were, and indeed are, ancient Greek editions of texts of Jewish origin which sometimes comprise more books, and sometimes give quite a different text. One of these Greek editions was accepted by most Christians of the first century and recognized as 'the scriptures'; it is known as the Septuagint. For this reason among others, Christians today have differing views about the precise extent of the biblical canon, and sometimes they argue – to my mind too little – about what version of the 'Jewish Bible' really should be part of the Christian Bible: the Hebrew, the Greek, or – as I think – both. But really these differences are unimportant for us now, for they relate largely to what one could call the limits of the book. Within it there is something like a common Bible, and it is useful to look at that once again in the light of the theory of evolution.

The question with which we began is: if the theory of evolution is correct, do we do better to leave the scriptures out of it, or could they take on a new significance precisely in the light of this? Here I shall not allow myself to be blocked by the false dilemma 'evolutionism or creationism'; rather, I shall seek another approach and finally return briefly to the question of creation, which is being discussed at greater length in other contributions.

IV. A primal centre

The argument developed above under the title 'Brain, speech and writing' concentrated on the transfer of information in the binary opposition of 'cultural' and 'genetic' and led me to look for lines and passages in scripture which could play a role in this connection. This search was not difficult, and the passages very quickly grouped themselves on a clearly recognizable line.

The line is easily and clearly visible if we look for passages which command the handing down of information that is thought to be important. These passages usually use one of two complementary codes: 'establish in the memory (of following generations)' and 'recall'. In addition, while these passages relate to many different situations, strikingly, for all the differences, they refer without exception to one and the same basic report or one primal event which can and indeed must therefore be regarded as the fundamental report. Thus recollection of this is the primal recollection. Perhaps not the oldest, but certainly the most influential passage, relates to the feast of Passover or Easter; we know that the rite mentioned in it is still celebrated today at the Passover meal:

> And when your children say to you, 'What do you mean by this service?,' you shall say, 'It is the sacrifice of the Lord's Passover, for he passed over the houses of the people of Israel in Egypt, when he slew the Egyptians but spared our houses' (Exodus 12.26–28; cf. also 13.8–10).

This reference to the exodus, the deliverance in and from Egypt, is repeated on many occasions. It is impossible to quote all the passages here. However, anyone who wants to assess their weight should look them up and read them. Time and again the same thing is said, whether it is about the sabbath (Deuteronomy 5.12–15), or the Feast of Booths (Leviticus 23.39–43), about the sacrifice of everything that opens the womb (Exodus 13.14–16), or about observing the precepts of the Torah (Deuteronomy 6.20). So it is not surprising that the summary of these precepts in ten main rules begins like this:

> I am the Lord your God who brought you out of the land of Egypt, from the house of slavery (Exodus 20.2; Deuteronomy 5.6).

Two of these situations should be mentioned specifically here. The first is the sacrifice of the firstfruits at the temple, for which the following confession of faith is provided:

> A wandering Aramaean was my father, and he went down into Egypt and sojourned there, few in number; and there he became a nation, great, might and populous. And the Egyptians treated us harshly, and afflicted us, and laid upon us hard bondage. Then we cried to the Lord the God of our fathers, and the Lord heard our voice, and saw our affliction, our toil and our oppression; and the Lord brought us out of Egypt with a mighty hand and outstretched arm, with great terror, with signs and wonders; and he brought us into this place and gave us this land, a land flowing with milk and honey. And behold, now I bring the first of the fruit of the ground, which you, O Lord, have given me (Deuteronomy 26.5–10).

V. The foundation for a rule of conduct

The second text does not relate to a rite, but does relate to a rule of behaviour. The regulations which apply to the special care of foreigners, slaves, widows and orphans – i.e. for those who more than others represent the underside of the society of the time – are inseparably connected with the specific experiences of ancient Israel in Egypt. They are all mentioned at the Feast of Weeks:

> And you shall rejoice before the Lord your God, you and your son and your daughter, your manservant and your maidservant, the Levite who is within your towns, the foreigner, the widows and orphans who are among you, at the place which the Lord your God will choose, to make his name dwell there. You shall remember that you were a slave in Egypt; and you shall be careful to observe these statutes (Deuteronomy 16.11–2; see also Exodus 22.20; 23.9; Leviticus 19.34; Deuteronomy 5.12–15; 10.18–19; 15,15; 16.12; 24.17–24).

Now it is of decisive interest in connection with a functioning cultural transfer of information that this transfer is repeated with great regularity: the memory must be preserved and held fast; it must not be forgotten and is above all to be handed on to the coming generation. That leads to the fixed rite according to which – as I have already remarked – still today the youngest son present at the celebration of the Passover has to ask about the meaning of the rites, rules of behaviour and precepts. It is the youngest, because he must be regarded as the most important in the chain of successive generations. In addition to the passages on the Passover quoted above, see also Exodus 13.1–16 about the sacrifice of all the firstborn, and Leviticus 23.43 on the Feast of Booths and Deuteronomy 6.20 on observing the instructions of the Torah. If we add that in the books from Exodus to Deuteronomy the saying 'The Lord your God who brought you out of Egypt' or a comparable standard formula recurs, then it seems to me indisputable that we can and must see the liberation of oppressed Israel from the 'house of slavery in Egypt' as the primal experience and consciousness of faith of pre-Christian Israel.

This primal experience was not only stated repeatedly, but was also crystallized in a very brief passage, in the story of the revelation to Moses at the 'burning bush', which can be read in Exodus 3. Not only what Moses sees is important, but also what he hears from the voice from the fire which does not consume:

> I have seen the affliction of my people who are in Egypt and have heard their loud cry against their taskmasters. I know their sufferings, and I have come down to deliver them out of the hand of the Egyptians (Exodus 3.7–8).

Anyone who looks at all these passages will find little difficulty in discovering in this notion of God (which is impressed on the reader of the Bible time and again, above all by the books of Exodus, Leviticus and Deuteronomy) the core of the biblical revelation.

VI. Only 'survival of the fittest'?

Now what has this image of God to do with the theory of evolution? Anyone who keeps in mind what I have said and at the same time thinks again of the Darwinistic slogans can easily discover that. In my view, the core of the tradition which I have described is a supplement to the basic thesis of the theory of evolution, perhaps also a corrective. Certainly the survival of the strongest is unavoidable in evolution, but that does not mean that those who go under in the struggle for life are written off. On the contrary, there is not only deliverance and salvation also for them, but above all for them. So alongside the survival of the fittest (or in the face of them) comes the salvation of the weakest; this also in two complementary ways.

The first way is the manner in which YHWH reveals himself. He makes himself seen and heard as the God of oppressed men and women, as the God of those who experience injustice and call on him for help, relief and deliverance. That is the revelation which according to the narrative in Exodus 3 Moses received at the bush in the wilderness that burned but was not consumed. This revelation is experienced in the deliverance from Egypt, written on the memory and on most occasions handed on from father to son. So it becomes the cultural information of this people.

The second way is expressed differently. It has to do with the conduct of those who bear this memory in themselves as their most precious possession. The compassion and mercy which they themselves have been able to experience from YHWH have to be reflected in their conduct. It is the compassion for other men and women on the underside of society, represented in widows and orphans, slaves and foreigners. God's compassion for the weak is a reason to be merciful oneself. Indeed it says a great deal that the guidelines and rules of behaviour which we call 'the Ten Commandments' begin with this picture of YHWH.

VII. And the Second Testament?

'But,' I hear the Christian readers of this article object to my remarks, 'surely our Bible is far more the Second than the First Testament! And there are quite different things in that.' At first sight they are right. The Second Testament has quite a different foundation story, namely that of Jesus' life, death and resurrection, and of the community of those who follow him. But this difference is only superficial; on closer inspection the whole Testament appears in a different light. The stories of the Second Testament are based on a paradigm which relates to the memory of the liberation from Egypt.

The Gospels seek to show how the same God still has mercy on the losers, those who are disadvantaged in the struggle for life against the strongest. Both the stories which Jesus himself tells in the Gospels and the stories about his own life and death work this out in concrete terms. It is certainly not without reason that the picture of the 'good shepherd' – a combination of passages from John 10 and Luke 15 – became one of the metaphors which for centuries was dominant among the depictions of Jesus in graphic art. On his shoulders he carries the one stray lamb from Luke 15 for which he left the ninety-nine others – who did not need him – to their fate in order to turn completely to the one lamb threatened with destruction. At the same time the observer to whom the stories of the Bible have not become completely strange thinks of the shepherd who has given his life for the sheep (John 10).

Many other Gospel accounts which have penetrated deep into the Christian consciousness also have to do with this. I might mention the 'prodigal son', which in Luke 15 along with the parables of the lost drachmae and the lost sheep stands among the stories of care for the underdog. And the same is also true of the parable of the good Samaritan in Luke 10.

Many other stories which the four Gospels have preserved about Jesus are based on the same paradigm. Those who consider the many healings and exorcisms attributed to Jesus in the Gospels as demonstrations of his power have in my view failed to understand them properly; for example, they overlook the fact that almost always these actions are preceded by a cry for help, just as the cry of the Israelites preceded their liberation from Egypt. Finally, the same thing is true of Jesus' own death and his resurrection, which in their combination are *the* example and paradigm of the salvation of the weakest.

VIII. A brief postscript on the creation story

From here, then, once again I shall look back briefly on the creation story. I shall not discuss here either the relationship between creationism and evolutionism nor the question of God's creative power. So I return only with questions.

As I began to read in Exodus, Leviticus and Deuteronomy and looked back from there to the first chapters of Genesis, the question occurred to me whether – in our memory and in our confessions – we might give creation the same significance as the liberation and exodus from Egypt. It struck me that from Exodus to Deuteronomy, while the exodus is constantly recalled, the creation is not. Could it be possible that the exodus refers to direct experiences which have found expression in stories and rites, whereas the creation is derived from these experiences and more than the exodus is the fruit of theological considerations? Could that also explain the fact that even in the sacrifice of the first fruits of the harvest, the one who offers the sacrifice recalls the liberation from Egypt but not the creation or a natural event, although this would be the obvious thing to do?

Another quite different question follows from that. Is it not really strange that our classical Christian confessions of belief in the creation immediately lead on to Jesus: 'I believe in God, the Father almighty, creator of heaven and earth, and in Jesus Christ his only Son our Lord'? Would it not have been very natural between these two elements also to confess the Father 'who has heard the cry of Israel in Egypt and liberated the oppressed from the power of the oppressors'? Those are only questions. I shall not attempt an answer, or even a first attempt at one. Rather, this contribution will be open ended, perhaps like evolution.

Translated by John Bowden

* *The author originally wrote this article for a Dutch journal. Because of his imminent death he could not revise the text thoroughly for this journal. So the editors of the issue omitted or changed some passages which were only understandable in the Dutch context. Otherwise the article has been taken over unchanged, so to speak as the author's testament to* Concilium.

In memoriam

Bastiaan M. F. van Iersel SMM was born on 27 September 1924 in Heerlen, The Netherlands, and in 1943 entered the congregation of the Montfortans. He studied theology, was ordained priest in 1950 and continued his theological studies at the universities of Nijmegen (1950–53) and Leuven (1953–1954). He gained his doctorate in 1962 with a work on *'The Son' in the Synoptic Sayings of Jesus*. Then in Nijmegen he became in succession Lecturer in New Testament in 1966 and Professor in 1974. From 1975 on he performed important functions both at the university and in national research, and as a specialist advisor was very influential up to his death. From 1987 to 1990, the year in which he retired, he was Rector of the university. Van Iersel published around 450 scholarly articles in various languages. He was a member and at times chairman of the editorial bodies of a variety of scholarly journals including *Schrift* (1969–1980) and *Tijdschrift voor Theologie* (1969–1989). As an amateur poet, after 1990 he wrote three volumes of haikus. However, he devoted most energy to his New Testament studies, especially research into the Gospel of Mark. He regarded the publication of his commentary on Mark in several languages as the climax and fulfilment of his scholarly life.

Bas van Iersel also performed important activities in Dutch public life. For some years he was engaged in party politics. He was also chairman of a national judicial institution for preserving security, an institute from the blind, a college and a foundation for the further education of older people. In recognition of his merits in 1989 he was made a Knight of the Order of the Lion.

In addition to these many activities, from 1964 van Iersel was a member of *Concilium* and until 1996 one of those responsible for the discipline of exegesis. He was active in producing twenty-five issues. From 1984 he was a member of the Foundation. Until a few days before his death he supported us with his advice. For almost fifty years, Bas van Iersel fought a threatening illness with extreme discipline. On 7 July 1999, reconciled with his life and supported by many grateful friends – he departed from us. One of the best experts, the most committed and hard-working members for *Concilium*, has left us. We thank him with all our hearts and commend him to the goodness of God.

The Editors

Teilhard de Chardin: The Message

LODOVICO GALLENI

After some years of enthusiasm following the first, partly uncritical, reading of the works of the French Jesuit, quite a long phase of apparent oblivion set in. In reality these were years of often silent but extremely useful work, culminating in the congress devoted to the figure and work of Fr Teilhard which was held in May 1994 within the framework of the annual conference on Cosmos and Creation organized by Loyola College, Baltimore, and Georgetown University.[1]

I took part in this congress, devoting particular attention to the analysis of Teilhard's scientific works and in particular to the relationship between these works and the current debate on evolutionary mechanism. In this article, too, I shall therefore attempt to present Teilhard's work and in particular the perspectives which derive from it from a quite neglected point of view, namely an analysis of his scientific work. Too often it has been forgotten that during his long and active life Fr Teilhard was fundamentally a scientist, involved in field work and palaeontological, geological and palaeoanthropological research. So it seems to me that to survey the 'scientific' aspects of his life is fundamental also to understanding the perspective of his theological proposals.[2]

I. Vocation

On an important page of his journal, Teilhard recalls his vocation and that of Cardinal Newman. It consists fundamentally in the aim to reconciling with God all that is good and fine in modernity. 'Yes, *I would like to reconcile with God what is good in* the modern world, its scientific intuitions, its social appetites and its legitimate criticism.'[3]

This is basically a risky vocation, but not a new one. It runs right through the history of the church, it is often misunderstood and is the source of harsh actions on the part of the hierarchy towards those who seek to follow it. This too is a vital aspect of the life of Teilhard de Chardin, which becomes particularly hateful at the point when, having been forbidden during his lifetime to publish his theological writings, he was accused, when they were published posthumously, of a lack of theological clarity. But how could Teilhard achieve that if his writings were denied the basic source of clarity, i.e. that progressive development of the idea which can come only from free debate and free confrontation?[4]

At the time when he wrote those words in his diary Teilhard was a stretcher bearer in a French regiment during the First World War, but he had also done important work as a palaeontologist and was working on his doctoral thesis at the prestigious Paris laboratory of Marcellin Boule.[5] The war interrupted his scientific activity, but not of course his vocation, which was not only that of a priest but also that of a scientist, indeed a scientist involved in one of the fundamental disciplines of palaeontology, namely evolution. So the key points of Teilhard's intellectual commitment are clear: the fundamental aspect of modernity which interested him was evolution, evolution not only as an object of scientific research but as the particular way in which God created the universe.

There is also another important statement in the first volume of his diary: 'The adoption of the evolutionary form for the formation of the world entails a certain mode of appearance 'ex nihilo subjecti' and suggests that there is a profound *ontological reason* for this world.'[6]

II. The problem of evolution

From reflections on evolution, a particular mode of creation emerges which requires a new approach to theology. So it is appropriate to devote a few words to the problem of evolution. In fact the word evolution denotes a continual process of transformation and genealogical interdependence which extends throughout the sphere of living beings and then to all the universe. Thus the universe is a universe continually coming into being, the principal characteristic of which is the emergence of the new; therefore time leads to irreversible change. The historicity of events which theology fundamentally inserted into the course of humankind as a history of covenant and salvation thus extends to the whole of created reality.

But evolution also poses other problems. Basically, with Darwin another important element overwhelmingly enters the debate on evolution, that of the chance nature of the mechanisms. Evolution proceeds at least on a biological level, and, to use a happy expression of Teilhard de Chardin's, gropes its way among the effects of large numbers and causality.[7] And this is the basic philosophical essence of Darwin's proposal, which, as was rightly emphasized as early as the second half of the nineteenth century by St George Mivart,[8] implies a particular mode of creation that invades the field of metaphysics and poses curious questions for theology. The chance nature of the evolutionary mechanisms introduces a lack of necessity in the emergency of human beings in the universe; moreover the process of groping brings in its wake an 'imperfection' in the evolutionary mechanisms which has serious repercussions on the global view of the universe. This is because right from the beginning of life these mechanisms introduce some elements which are then sources of suffering, pain and death. These aspects are no longer the consequence of sin but form part of the very matter of the universe. Another happy expression of Teilhard's sums up the problem: 'Thousands of centuries before a first thinking being appeared on our earth, life was swarming, with its instincts, passions, pains and deaths.'[9]

So the change which is required of theology is a major one; in fact we no longer find ourselves confronted with a universe which already emerged complete and ordered from the hands of the creator and thus is immediately the sign of a divine order and perfection, and is entrusted to humankind. At this point humankind can only respect the existing order or alter it with its sin, leading to negative factors like pain, suffering and death.

The new vision is that of a universe which is making itself in time, in which what counts is not so much the order that existed in the past but the self-organization which will be concentrated on the future. And here it is again worth devoting some attention to the evolutionary mechanisms.

Today, in fact, there is no longer any doubt about the phenomenon of evolution. We can in fact state that now the evolution of living beings is the result of a historical investigation which has provided as much proof as there is proof for the existence of the Roman empire. Indeed, although the proofs for the existence of the Roman empire are indirect proofs, like discoveries of a historical kind or the study of its consequences in the present, like, for example, the spread of the neo-Latin languages, no one denies their historical reality. The same goes for evolution, in which we have discoveries of a historical kind, for example fossils, and consequences in the present, like the current diffusion of living species, the profound unity of the mechanisms of life and the relationships of affinity which bring together living beings themselves in a decisively univocal way. So no one should or can deny the historical reality of evolution either.

Evolution, understood as the transformation of living beings in time, becomes the guiding structure of the experimental sciences of our century, which extends from biology to physics and thus from life to the whole universe. So it is a fact that it has an ontological value and that it represents a particular mode of creation which raises questions for theology and which theology can no longer ignore. The great merit of Teilhard has been that he posed the problem seriously, as is evident from the page of the journal that I have just cited.

This could be the point to raise an epistemological question, namely how science has the instruments also to ascertain, in its work, facts which have an ontological value, but to discuss that would take us too far afield. Here I shall limit myself to critical realism, namely the present-day epistemology which begins from one of the open tracks of Popperian reflection and, which while recognizing that science works by theories, paradigms and programmes of research that can be falsified, revised and integrated, and are thus constantly subject to criticism and revision and can be outdated, nevertheless recognizes that science comes up against a reality that exists and is knowable, and therefore also succeeds in giving definitive information with an ontological value of which theology must therefore take account.[10]

III. From the ordered universe to the earth to be constructed

So Teilhard belongs in that tradition of theological reflection which sees the work of science as an instrument for understanding the way in which God works in creation and which therefore considers science as a fundamental instrument for understanding the projects that are sometimes written in the book of revelation in a way which is not immediate and universal; an instrument which stands alongside and is integrated with that which derives from the study of revelation.[11]

What, however, is peculiar is that here we find ourselves in the cultural sphere of a science which works in fields decisive for the study of biological evolution, which proposes important theories from a scientific perspective, theories which moreover were also strongly influenced by Teilhard's personal vision, to which theology was clearly by no means alien, which in the end also constructed a synthesis not only of disciplines but also of languages,[12] and which represents a proposal for an integration of the fact of evolution into theology.

We can consider as the starting point of Teilhard's construction the metaphysical idea of 'moving towards'. This is an idea which derives from the surrounding French culture, since basically it fits well with the Lamarckian concept of progress that stands behind the construction of the first theory of evolution.[13] And Lamarckian progress suggested to Teilhard the more general idea that evolution did not choose as it were by chance the line which leads to human beings and therefore to conscious reflection and to the noosphere (to use his term) as the fortunate outcome of many possibilities.[14] On the contrary, this is the result of mechanisms which are experimental and which in some way take account of the evolutionary way towards thought.

From this point of view it is fundamental to note how this direction in research already emerges in experimental works published at the beginning of the 1920s and devoted to the palaeontology of mammals. In one of the works which report the studies he made for his doctoral thesis, on the 'Primates of the Phosphorites of Quercy',[15] Teilhard clearly brings out the line which leads to cerebralization, showing how it is possible to hypothesize parallelisms in the various evolutionary lines from the primates that can be interpreted as an experimental demonstration of the presence of a tendency towards cerebralization.

At this point the first important point of contact between the theological view and scientific investigation emerges, namely 'moving towards'. And in fact, as I have said, it is true that while evolution, at least in part, presents decisively chance mechanisms, on the whole lines, parallelisms and canalizations emerge which are the experimental reflection of this general evolutionary characteristic of 'moving towards'.

Teilhard continued to develop this line throughout his long and busy scientific activity. Here the Chinese period becomes important in which, as well as becoming the founder of modern palaeontology of the vertebrates of this geographical area and also one of the members of the research group working on the remains of so-called Peking Man, Teilhard understood the need to extent the study of evolutionary phenomenon to the continental dimension. This is an important transition, because it goes beyond the limited investigation of a restricted area of the population, which was the basic activity, by engaging in the re-reading of Darwinism taking place at that time which went under the name of 'the modern synthesis'.[16]

According to Teilhard, once the evolution of a group is studied over long periods and vast spaces, it loses the distortions which arise from the action of forces acting locally and brings out the internal rhythm that characterizes it. This approach is well exemplified, experimentally, by Teilhard's studies of the mole-rat of the Chinese Pleistocene, the evolution of which, studied over long periods and broad areas, is in effect characterized by phenomena of parallelisms and canalizations.

To study these aspects Teilhard now proposed a new science, geobiology, dedicated to the study of continental evolution. This was considered a better way of studying evolution on a broader level, and seen as the ultimate object of the study of the biosphere, which evolves as a single complex entity. This instrument is the most important result, from the scientific viewpoint, of his intuition of a general movement in the evolution of the universe towards complexity and consciousness; it enables a demonstration of the tendency towards cerebralization, at least at the level of animal evolution.[17]

At this point we have two important instruments at our disposal. On the one hand, evolution presents a characteristic which can be the object of experimental research and which is the 'movement towards' cerebralization. This allows us to state that the biosphere, evolving towards a single complex unity, 'moves towards' the conscious creature and thus towards the noosphere. On the other hand this 'moving towards' also take place by means of tentative mechanisms, which are not strictly deterministic or necessarily ordered towards a goal. Basically, this too is an important consequence of the evolutionary view of life and poses questions for theological reflection. Ours is not an ordered world, the mechanisms of which work in a precise and strictly deterministic manner, resulting in the birth of humankind; the order is in the future, and it is an order that is constructed. Now if the order is constructed, it is clear that at the start there must be a broad sphere of disorder to organize, of limits and thresholds to overcome, of dishomogeneity in structures. Basically the indeterminacy present in evolutionary mechanisms is a reflection of the autonomy with which matter organizes itself and is also the biological sign of a greater value, namely the philosophical and theological value of freedom. The universe constructs itself in freedom and autonomy. But the canalizations, the parallelisms, the 'moving towards' at any rate guarantee within these spaces of freedom and autonomy the emergence of the thinking creature and thus of the noosphere. So 'moving towards' and freedom are two strong elements in the Teilhardian approach.

But there is a third fundamental element, which is that of 'constructing the earth'. I have just spoken of a disorder to be organized in a perspective of freedom within a general 'movement towards' freedom. But this raises another important problem, that of pain, suffering and death. In a more traditional theological perspective, in a literal reading, for example, of the texts of the Council of Trent, suffering, pain and death entered the world as a consequence of sin.[18] Basically, here again we have the fixed approach (useful to science but in reality disastrous for theology) which sees a universe that emerges ordered by the hands of God down to the smallest detail and that human intervention can change only for the worse. But reflection in an evolutionary perspective requires us to approach the problem in a completely different way. As I have said, suffering, pain, death are characteristics of life and are closely connected with the very matter of the universe.

The way out is thus to 'construct' the earth, but this also raises other problems, first of all precisely what it means to 'construct' the earth and finally to what degree.

The theological value of 'constructing' the earth is connected with the rediscovery of an eschatological perspective also within terrestrial reality. In fact the eschatological perspective does not consist in thinking of the future of individuals beyond this earth who therefore have to be preoccupied with the salvation of their own souls, basically disinterested in what happens to the rest of humanity. Involvement in earthly reality, when it is present, is seen only as an instrument of personal salvation. With Teilhard the perspective is boldly integrated, and to the road upwards to paradise is also added the way forwards to 'construct' the earth, that earth made up of human beings, but also of animals and plants, rocks and waters, which thus also acquire a value in the eschatological perspective. The 'constructed' earth and the humanity which has constructed it rightly are the necessary conditions for the second coming of Christ. The 'moving towards' brought about by the thinking creature with the correct use of freedom and in the perspective of 'constructing' the earth thus ends in the grandiose final perspective of the Omega Point: the moment of the second coming of Christ.[19]

Of course it is not for the scientist to take this course, which is so peculiarly Teilhardian; however, what does have to be emphasized is the need to show how the course of evolution has a final goal which is added to the salvation history of individuals and becomes the history of the salvation not only of all humanity but also of the biosphere, to which all humankind has given its origin and with which it is profoundly connected.

In Teilhard's perspective, to the traditional way upwards typical of ultra-terrestrial eschatology is added a way forwards, for the salvation of earth and humankind on earth, which acquires all the force of its direct contact with the themes of evolutionary biology and the concrete nature of the study of fossils and stones.

Basically, we cannot fail to see here, too, in a future opening up to eschatology of the biosphere, another of the themes characteristic of the present-day debate between science and theology. In other words, it is now for science to develop its own apocalyptic with scenarios of the end of the world, either in the distant but fascinating prospect of the end of the universe, or in that nearer prospect which preoccupies us, of the end of the biosphere or at least of the higher forms of life because of the progressive destruction which humankind is bringing about on earth.[20]

And here the ultimate perspective emerges. It is important to 'construct' the earth, to allow the eschatological perspective of the Omega Point. But there is something else to consider, which is strongly connected with Teilhard's scientific experience. The study of evolution in depth is not just research into the past of humankind but is also an important indication for extrapolations into the future.[21] The mechanisms of evolution are such as to have guaranteed the stability of the biosphere and thus the survival of a protected space in which it has been possible for life to evolve and to realize its characteristic movement towards the thinking being. But in that case, in 'constructing' the earth the thinking being must first of remember to work within the parameters which have allowed the stability of the biosphere and have been consolidated in the course of the evolution of Life. The study of evolution shows not only how many spaces there have been for 'constructing' the earth and how broad they have been, but also the great risks run by humanity when it leaves these space or actually ruins relations and mechanisms which have now been consolidated.

However, there are ample possibilities within these mechanisms for the human action of 'constructing' an earth which God enjoyed on the seventh day. The seventh day is the day of God's rest, because now the creation has been entrusted to the work of the creature who thinks and is free. Here Teilhard's message has been brought up to date in the perspective suggested by Moltmann,[22] which is probably the most mature and fascinating development of Teilhard's theological approaches.

For Moltmann, once the thinking creature appeared, God could rest and enjoy the creation finally entrusted to the care of humanity, which builds it in a covenant with the creator.

From this perspective the problems of so-called original sin[23] are also fully covered: the creature has to construct the earth, bringing that order which is not present from the beginning, increasing the harmony of what has been created and at least in part removing the limits of the 'movement towards' creation, i.e. those fortuitous and causal aspects which in part are one of the sources of pain and suffering in nature. This can be done if the continuous and constant covenant with the creator is emphasized up to the beginning of the human adventure. But this has not happened and the covenant has been rejected, not so much in a single episode, as in the biblical narrative, but because of the way which humanity has really followed for a long time in rejecting the covenant. The dramatic aspects of the mechanisms of evolution not only have not been alleviated or removed, but have even been accentuated.

Another terrible force of evil has entered the universe, that of the thinking and free creature which is the cause of pain and death for other thinking and free creatures of the destruction of nature. And the greatest point of negation of the covenant is that of the distorted use of liberty, which is arrived at when creatures use their freedom to kill, even, their creator. It is here, then, that to the story of the way without the covenant and of the covenant finally accepted by Abraham is also added the way of salvation and redemption which comes from the cross. But all this, in the new Teilhardian approach, and also in the eschatological perspective bound up with 'constructing' the earth,[24] evidently takes on a new dimension or at least a new reading, which opens up into the synthesis between science and theology, or at any rate between the biblical perspective and the vision of a universe in evolution.

Translated by John Bowden

Notes

1. The proceedings of the meeting have been published in an issue of *Zygon* edited by James F. Salmon and entitled *Pierre Teilhard de Chardin Revisited, Zygon* 30.1, March 1995.
2. L. Galleni, 'Relationships between Scientific Analysis and the World View of Pierre Teilhard de Chardin', *Zygon* 27.2, 153–6; id., 'How does the Teilhardian Vision of Evolution Compare with Contemporary Theories?', *Zygon* 30.1, 1995, 25–45.
3. In P. Teilhard de Chardin, *Journal,* Vol.1, Paris 1975, 90. The italics are in the text.
4. As an example of this attitude, reference could be made to the comment of the *Osservatore romano* on the publication of the note from the Holy Office on 30 June 1962.
5. Cf. Pierre Teilhard de Chardin, 'Les carnassiers des phosphorites du Quercy', *Annales de Paléontologie* IX, 1914–1915, 13–90; reprinted in *Pierre Teilhard de Chardin, L'oeuvre scientifique*, ed. Nicole and Karl Schmitz Moorman, Olten and Freiburg im Breisgau 1971, 189–197.
6. Teilhard de Chardin, *Journal*, Vol.1 (n.3), 264. Italics in the text.
7. Cf. P. Teilhard de Chardin, *L'apparition de l'homme*, Paris 1956.
8. St George Jackson Mivart (1827–1900) is another of the dramatic figures in the debate on evolution. An English zoologist, but close to Newman in his religious views, he tried to engage in a serious discussion of both the scientific aspects of Darwinism and their impact on the theology of creation in his book, St George

Mivart, *On the Genesis of Species*, London 1871. As a result he was harshly attacked by English scientific circles close to Darwin, but also ended up being excommunicated by the Catholic Church.

9. P. Teilhard de Chardin, *Comment je crois*, Paris 1969.
10. For critical realism see the works of K. R. Popper. Other relevant texts are A. R. Peacocke, *Theology for a Scientific Age*, London and Minneapolis 1993,1–24; W. van Huyssteen, *Theology and the Justification of Faith*, Grand Rapids 1989, 24–190; D. Lambert, *Science et théologie*, Namur 1999, 26–35; L. Galleni, *Scienza e Teologia*, Brescia 1992, 15–35.
11. Basically it still starts from Galileo's position in the Copernican Letters, cf. Galileo Galilei, *Le lettere copernicane*, Rome 1995.
12. It is perhaps worth remembering that the synthesis is that reported in P. Teilhard de Chardin, *The Phenomenon of Man*, London 1955.
13. For the concept of progress in connection with evolution and the evolutionists see M. Ruse, *Monad to Man, The Concept of Progress in Evolutionary Biology,* Cambridge, Mass. 1990. However, the volume has serious limitations because it trivializes the presence of Teilhard de Chardin in the evolutionary debate. This is a further sign of the mistrust that his work has evoked, among other things because it is almost totally unknown, at least as far as its scientific results are concerned.
14. As examples of this attitude see J. Monod, *Chance and Necessity*, London 1970, and Stephen Jay Gould, *Wonderful Life,* New York 1989.
15. P. Teilhard de Chardin, 'Sur quelques primates des phosphories du Quercy', *Annales de Paléontologie*, 1916–1921, 1–20, reprinted in *Pierre Teilhard de Chardin, L'oeuvre scientifique* (n.5), 221–45.
16. In this connection see J. Huxley, *Evolution. The Modern Synthesis,* London 1942.
17. P. Teilhard de Chardin, 'Géobiologie et Géobiologia', *Geobiologia* 1, 1943, 1–8, reprinted in *Pierre Teilhard de Chardin, L'oeuvre scientifique* (n.5), 3753–60.
18. Cf. Galleni, *Scienza e Teologia* (n.10), 77–90.
19. L. Galleni, 'La realtà ontologica dell'evoluzione: dall universo ordinato alla terra fa costruire', in *Prismi di verità*, ed, M. Malaguti, Rome 1997, 141–66.
20. In this connection see e.g. I. Sanna, *Fede, Scienza e fine del mondo*, Brescia 1996.
21. Cf. Kino Conti, 'Teilhard de Chardin e la prevedibilità del fenomenon evolutivo', *Annali della Facoltà di Lettere e Filosofia, Università di Perugia* 4, 32, 1995, 343–402.
22. J. Moltmann, *God in Creation*, London 1985.
23. Cf. G. Martelet, *Libre réponse à un scandale*, Paris 1986.
24. At this point we are inevitably reminded, as logical developments of Teilhard's perspective, of some terms from liberation theology (cf. L. Boff, *Cry of the Earth, Cry of the Poor*, Maryknoll, NY 1996), feminist theology (R. Radford Ruether, *Gaia and God,* London and San Francisco 1992) and contextual theology (cf. A. Potente, *Raccogliere i frammenti,* Rome 1995).

Sri Aurobindo. An Encounter between East and West

THOMAS AYKARA

I. Person and perspective

Sri Aurobindo, philosopher and mystic, poet and critic, was one of the most outstanding Indian thinkers of the twentieth century. A many-sided genius of extensive knowledge and intense mystical experience, Aurobindo was greeted already in 1928 by his fellow Indian Nobel Prize winner Rabindranath Tagore with the words: 'India will speak through your voice to the world.' And indeed he did speak, offered a magnificent message and proposed an integrated synthesis of the Eastern and the Western world. Sri Aurobindo (1872–1950), born Indian, brought up British, had throughout his life taught man's spiritual growth and eventual transformation leading to the emergence of a Supermind, a thought surprisingly similar to that proposed by the French scientist–mystic, Teilhard de Chardin. By training they were a classicist and a paleontologist respectively, but their thoughts met and merged to a great extent in their emergent mysticism.

Aurobindo's intuitive intellect, combined with his yogic experiences of deep mystical dimensions, was able to produce a number of remarkable works in prose and poetry that will become increasingly relevant to the human predicament in the third millennium. We are at a crucial crossroads of our evolutionary progress, our emerging destiny, that we alone can determine. The divergence between knowledge and wisdom has grown increasingly dangerous with every new technological innovation. Human beings have power in abundance; whether they have the wisdom to use that power for creative rather than destructive purposes is still a crucial question. We all have, in the words of William James, reservoirs of life to draw upon, of which we do not dream. Human attempts at development must be coupled with creative dreams. Though there are encouraging signs that the movement towards integration and world harmony is gathering momentum, there is even more alarming evidence that human folly has by no means exhausted itself. Kosovo and Kashmir are the latest examples. We must realize that might and material superiority alone cannot bring about human harmony and integral growth. Harmony cannot be created by anybody from outside. It must evolve from within. In this context Aurobindo's synthesis of integral evolution, with his glowing promise of a new leap in the very texture of consciousness, stands as a pathfinder towards brighter dawns of the future, and a prophetic contribution towards the building up of a new humanity.

Both Eastern and Western thought meaningfully meet in Aurobindo. In his vision evolution and faith are so intimately intertwined in the very depth of reality that every step in the evolution of the universe is a progressive growth in consciousness. This encounter is not in externals but in essentials, and prophetically inspirational. He aims at a real synthesis. Prophetic thinker and profound mystic as he was, Aurobindo was a real discoverer, a discoverer of profound proportion and dimensions of the Spirit. He was a scientist of the Spirit, who laid bare the supranatural level of consciousness, thus opening up an immense realm of spiritual experience. Having attained a perfect silence of the mind, he had no need to think, so he claimed, but only to write down in terms of intellect all that he had discovered and come to know in practising his integral yoga. His creative discoveries, deeply rooted in his profound mystical experiences of the inner unity of Reality, enabled him to journey in the realms of consciousness leading to an ideal fulfilment of what both the East and the West ardently aspired for. The West naturally aims at a fuller realization of the evolutionary and cosmic nature of its thought. But exaggerated intellectualism and a one-sided analytical approach has apparently fragmented its vision, compartmentalized its thought and hampered its inner evolutionary progress. Eastern thought in general and Indian thought in particular is more spiritual in nature and mostly individualistic in its preoccupations. Both have to transcend their cultural limitations and experiential constraints and aim at an evolutionary fulfilment. Sri Aurobindo tried in his own unique way to fulfil this function by concentrating more on two threads of his thought: the question of evolution and the function of integral yoga.

II. Evolution reinterpreted

The fact of evolution is accepted today by all scientists. Their interpretations are evidently different and the evolutionary theory is still developing. The history of evolution is a process of disclosure of reality over millennia, which, however, is still open to the future and which – if human beings do not destroy themselves and their world – will reach further dimensions of reality, but at the same time will come up against new limits to knowledge.[2] Aurobindo accepted the cosmic view of evolution of the West but rejected its mechanical character and tried to replace it by a spiritual evolution. Similarly, he rejected the cyclical view of Indian thought and the individualistic outlook of its theory of evolution and replaced it by the cosmic and personal outlook of the West. Consequently he reinterpreted the theory of evolution and replaced it by a spiritual evolution, an evolution in integration culminating in final convergence. His theory of evolution is based on a fundamental intuition that human beings have an acute sense of aspiration, which manifests itself in the divination of the Godhead. It is an inner impulse towards, an innate search after, a sense of a secret immortality. At the heart of this existential aspiration is the mutable Becoming of the immutable Being, a self-projection of Brahman into the conditions of space and time. He turns the traditionally miserable man into a magnificent mutable becoming of the infinite essence of the Absolute. Man becomes the incarnation of the Logos, the expression of the creative power; the Absolute becomes involved in matter. His deep mystical experiences coupled with his adherence to Hindu Scriptures *(anubhava* and *Śruti)* made him develop a theory of evolution that was essentially spiritual in character. Consequently evolution becomes a spiritual process and a dialectic of descent and ascent. The ultimate driving force and the ground of evolution is the power of the Spirit that is operative in its dynamic infolding and unfolding in matter. That there is no part of reality which is not in some degree infused with the absolute Spirit is another basic intuition on which he develops his doctrine of evolution.

III. The encounter between East and West in evolution

The idea of evolution is certainly more prominent in Western philosophy than in Indian philosophy. Greek philosophy gives it considerable importance. In Aristotle, evolution was more teleological. Plotinus' theory of emanation has some outward similarity with Aurobindo's understanding of Divine Involution. The individual souls in Plotinus' thought undoubtedly realize God both as the immanent principle working within and also as the transcendent Source which the individual can reach by a long progression, through a series of stages. But in Aurobindo's thought, both these immanent and transcendent aspects are kept well in mind from the very beginning. Even in the lowest forms of matter, the Absolute is present as an indwelling principle, as in the language of the Bhagavad Gita, the most popular scripture of Hinduism, a dweller within the heart pushing it continually forward. The Absolute is everywhere, writes Aurobindo; it has to be seen and found everywhere. Every finite is an infinite and has to be known and sensed in its intrinsic infiniteness as well as in its surface finite appearance.[3]

Aurobindo rejects the *Advaita* (monism) of Śankara, for he asserts unity to the detriment of multiplicity. Ramanuja's *Viśiṣṭādvaita* (qualified monism) denies the unqualified oneness and unity of the Absolute and Madhava' s *Dvaita* (dualism) fails to recognize unity in the multiple. It was to correct and complete these three prominent schools in Indian thought that he developed his theory of integral evolution and integral yoga in which transcendence and immanence meet in human transformation, a gradual spiritual evolution. It is the involution of the Absolute in matter that makes this spiritual evolution inevitable. The appearance of human mind and body on earth marks a crucial step, a decisive change in the course and process of evolution. The human ability to know ourselves is a significant step to the ascent to that perfect self-transparency of the Absolute. Thus Aurobindo sees that there can be a higher status of consciousness than this present one, a state beyond the realm of the mental. The final goal he envisages is a spiritual age, a birth of a new consciousness, an upward revolution of the human being, a descent of the Spirit in our members, a spiritual reorganization of our life.

Drawing inspiration mostly from Greek thought, the West formulated different interpretations of evolution down through the centuries. The Greek mind directed its attention first to the outward, and only at a later stage was it directed inwards. The Indian mind, on the contrary, turned inwards right from the very beginning. The highest reality was always conceived as *Atman* or Self. Consequently the interpretation of the universe was always in terms of consciousness. The progressive disclosures of reality are in evolving stages of consciousness. The creative evolution of Henri Bergson and the organic and emergent evolution of Whitehead have some striking similarities with Aurobindo: the former are materialistic in outlook whereas Aurobindo's is spiritualistic in essence. The key to the understanding of the sources and nature of evolution is not to be found in the organic process of nature but is to be sought in the Ultimate Reality, the ground and goal of All, incessantly converging to the One.

Modern humankind with its magnificent achievements and progress is undergoing an evolutionary crisis. We are still only human animals, says Aurobindo.[4] Our central will of life is still situated in our vital and physical being; we are enlightened but not yet transformed. If humankind is to survive, a radical transformation of human nature is necessary. Religions and regulations, teachers and treatises, all these have not succeeded in bringing about this indispensable transformation. They often concentrate more on transcendence at the expense of transformation; an other-worldly transcendence that does not pay sufficient attention to human existential strains and struggles. In spite of their extraordinary achievements, human beings today stand fragmented and frustrated. They have to cease to be mere human animals; they have to begin to be supreme human spirits. It is to achieve this new consciousness or new stage of spiritual being that Aurobindo introduces his discipline of yoga.

IV. Yoga made integral

The synthesis of the inner and the outer, the Teilhardian 'within' and 'without', heaven and earth, One and Many, is the central objective of Aurobindo's integral yoga. It is to justify this objective that he repeatedly appeals to the principle of intermediaries. After asserting categorically the essential identity of matter and spirit, Aurobindo establishes the 'law of intermediaries' that is to rule the progressive evolution of the Spirit in matter. Already from time immemorial the Upanishadic teaching said: energize the conscious energy in you, for the Energy is Brahman. The eternal spirit is not merely an inhabitant of this bodily mansion, but the very matter is a fit and noble material out of which he weaves constantly his garbs, builds recurrently the unending series of his mansions, for 'Matter also is Brahman'. Behind the appearance there is an identity in essence of these two extreme modes of existence, matter and spirit. It is in human consciousness that this reconciliation starts, emerges and achieves its goal of integration and convergence. The extension and emergence of this consciousness, to be satisfying, must necessarily be an inner enlargement from the individual to the cosmic existence. This cosmic existence is the final goal of man in his evolutionary journey in consciousness, of which *Sachchidananda* (Existence – Consciousness – Bliss) is the beginning, the middle and the end, the ground and the goal.

Supermind, a unique concept that Aurobindo introduces as the constitutive bridge between matter and spirit, nature and supernature, is the important medium between the *Sachchidananda* and his external manifestations, the unfolding universe of matter – life – mind. This is, therefore, one eternal and infinite Being, but seven distinguishable terms of Being or the sevenfold cord of Being, as Aurobindo would express it. It is the Supermind that develops the triune principle of existence, consciousness and bliss out of their indivisible unity. Aurobindo's unique interpretation of Supermind as the inherent and incessantly transformative power of *Sachchidananda* plays a key role in his understanding of evolution in terms of stages in consciousness. It is a principle of active will and knowledge superior to mind and creative of the worlds. It is the mediating power and state of being between that self-possession of the One and this flux of the many. Supermind is the vast self-extension of the Brahman that contains and develops. Supermind bridges the gap between reason and mystery, and combines the impersonal Being, personal God and individual self into three inseparable and equally real modes of the Supreme Reality. The hierarchical stages of mind leading to Supermind are typically expressed in particular kinds of extraordinary activity – higher mind in synoptic thought, illumined mind in mystical inspiration, intuitive mind in religious genius and overmind in world-transforming action – while Supermind has yet to come down and transform our planet. The rational justification of his integral yoga depends on the doctrine of Supermind whose presence and power he discovers at the very root of man's basic aspiration. His search from the aspiring human–animal leads him to a transparent Supermind who is to be realized in the new consciousness that awaits man. This is the final goal of his journey in human consciousness. Aurobindo made use of the path of integral yoga to realize this goal.

Aurobindo, like the sages of the East, firmly believed that awareness is the door to realization. There is above all the authentic divine dynamism, capable of transforming human nature and creating a new world order. This transformation is made possible through an ascent of consciousness towards the Infinite and final descent of the Infinite into the finite. But human beings are unfortunately wrapped up in manifold ignorance of which they have first of all to become conscious. Awareness of the ignorance that we are in is the beginning of human wisdom and progress. The more we become aware of the limits of our knowledge, the nearer we are to wisdom and true knowledge. The reason and root of our inbuilt ignorance is our alienation from the divine consciousness. This is overcome only through Yoga, the integral union with the divine. The integral yoga of Aurobindo assimilates the triple paths of Bhagavad Gita and aims at total human transformation, body and soul, an integral and radical transformation. A synthesis of all the yogas implies an integration of all the dimensions of human being, including bodily existence. The human being stands for a complete synthesis, integral fulfilment, the supra-mental synthesis that indeed fulfils the supreme quest of the human soul.

V. The significance of Aurobindo's synthesis

Aurobindo's synthesis is intelligible only in the context of his understanding of Reality as One in All and All in One. His creative vision of integrating the interiority and transcendence in human beings as becoming beings is very significant in the East–West encounter. The scientific rigour of the analytical mind in the West has to be coupled with and supported by the testimony of experience as the expressions of the inner Spirit. The entire person with its physical, psychic and spiritual potentialities is in process, a mutual constitutive process of inner encounter between the mutable becoming of the immutable Being. Human beings' power of self-transcendence is the pivot of their further evolution, their attitude of 'unselfing' (in the language of Iris Murdoch). All cultures have countless records of men and women who have displayed these powers in terms of physical, mental and spiritual capacities. This is supported by present-day studies in medical science, physical research, psychological sciences and comparative religious studies. As far as the natural scientists are concerned, writes Hans Küng, the evolution process as such neither includes nor excludes the origin and the goal. But they cannot ignore the basic question of origin, meaning and goal of the whole process. We have to choose between the groundlessness or meaninglessness of Jacques Monod or – on the lines of Manfred Eigen – the primordial ground or primordial meaning of everything.[6] There seems to be a broad agreement emerging that the human nature is undergoing further evolutionary development. Aurobindo's prophetic synthesis becomes extremely significant in the light of humankind's adventurous explorations into the future evolution of human nature.

Aurobindo's integration of matter and spirit, evolution and faith, situated and synchronized at the very heart of human consciousness, and saturated by his mystical experiences, can make a considerable contribution towards the shaping of a more relevant theology. Having long been alienated from the mystical, mythical and cosmic levels of human consciousness, the theologians of the future must open themselves to their depth and power, and integrate their resources into the faith, lived out daily, in which they encounter in concrete form the human consciousness of God. The emergent mysticism of Aurobindo, constitutively integrating unity in diversity, can possibly inspire theologians to create a more open and assimilative theology, especially in the field of theology of religious pluralism. It is by analysing human beings' living and growing consciousness, by reintegrating it into its relational and complementary setting, that the theologians and theologies of the future can make more creative contributions.

VI. Conclusion

The evolutionary mysticism of Sri Aurobindo is naturally over-optimistic. While constantly concentrating on the encounter between matter and spirit, Aurobindo did not give sufficient attention to the human problem of evil and misery in the world. Though conversant with some schools of psychology, he does not seem to be sufficiently informed of the scientific findings of modern psychological sciences. Perhaps he attached too much importance to his doctrine of Supermind. He was a prophet of the Spirit rather than a scientist of matter. But his integration of matter and Spirit in an emergent consciousness in human beings is a creative contribution towards a meaningful encounter between the Eastern and Western world and a remarkable guide in the march to our destiny. The balance between unity and diversity is the hallmark of his emerging integration realized in the inner encounter. This integration enlightens us on how to escape from the existential estrangements within ourselves and among our fellow human beings, and finally on how to escape estrangement from the Divine.

The innermost aspiration moving dynamically from within us is a perennial source of strength to go forward and an ever-abiding hope that makes human beings look forward to a life beyond. Trust anchored in the permeating presence of the Spirit in us and the hope hidden at the heart of reality is the dynamic source of evolution and the unfailing strength of faith. From a Christian perspective, this inbuilt trust and the consequent hope will make the risen images of Christ broader and brighter for us, pilgrims on this planet.

Notes

1. Thomas Aykara, *Cosmic Consciousness. A Comparative Study on Teilhard de Chardin and Sri Aurobindo*, Bangalore 1997, 143.
2. Hans Küng, *Eternal Life? Life After Death as a Medical, Philosophical and Theological Problem*, New York and London 1985, 223–4.
3. Sri Aurobindo, *Synthesis of Yoga*, Centenary Edition Vol. XX, Pondicherry 1972, 375.
4. Ibid., 408.
5. Michael Murphy, *Explorations into the Future Evolution of Human Nature*, Los Angeles 1992.
6. Küng, *Eternal Life* (n.2).

DOCUMENTATION

Theology and Science in Dialogue

PALMYRE M. F. OOMEN

Although connections between faith/theology and science were already being sought in the nineteenth century, the main impression given is that in this century the division between the two domains was the predominant factor. That gradually changed in the twentieth century.

After some pioneers like Karl Heim and Pierre Teilhard de Chardin had taken the initiative, a cautious openness to 'nature' developed among some theologians. That was a more obvious development in Catholic theology with its traditional emphasis on creation (one might mention, for example, Karl Rahner and Paul Overhage), but on the Protestant side, too, the theme of nature was rediscovered as a theological theme and discussed at length by individual theologians (Johannes M. de Jong, Wolfhart Pannenberg and later Jürgen Moltmann). However, for a long time there was no broad theological reflection on the insights of the natural sciences either on the Protestant or on the Catholic side. Still, from the 1960s one can speak of a rise of initiatives worldwide on the relationship between faith/theology and science and intensive thought on the issue (if this, too, can be described as 'broad').

All over the world a large number of institutions and individuals are occupied with the relationship between faith/theology and the natural sciences. Detailed information about them can be found in *Who's Who in Theology and Science*, compiled and edited by the John Templeton Foundation, New York: Continuum Publishing Co 1996 (713 pp.).

Here are some of the institutions, in alphabetical order:

Het Bezinningscentrum (Interdisciplinary Centre of the Study of Science, Society and Religion)
Het Bezinningscentrum, a centre at the Free University (Amsterdam, the Netherlands), stimulates research on the relationship between science (including humanities) and religion. The centre organizes public events, such as lectures, and bears editorial responsibility for many monographs. One of its sections concerns the

relationship between theology and the natural sciences. The director of this section is Prof. Dr Willem B. Drees.
Website: <http://www.vu.nl/Bezinningscentrum>

The Centre for Interdisciplinary Studies in Cracow
This centre is located at the Pontifical Academy of Theology in Cracow, Poland. Since the late 1970s Prof. Dr Michael Heller and Prof. Dr Joseph Zycinski have continued several research programmes in the field of the science–faith dialogue, especially on modern cosmology and the problem of creation, evolution theory, and various historical problems.
Address: Pontifical Academy of Cracow, Bernardynska 3, 31069 Kraków, Poland.

The Center for Theology and the Natural Sciences (CTNS)
CTNS is a non-profit international membership organization dedicated to research, teaching and public service. It is an affiliate of the Graduate Theological Union at Berkeley, California. The mission of CTNS is to promote the creative mutual interaction between the contemporary natural sciences (physics, cosmology, technology, environmental studies, evolutionary and molecular biology) and contemporary Christian theology and ethics. The mission is deployed through three objectives: research, education and public service. CTNS has intensive co-operation with the Vatican Observatory in a research programme (lasting ten years) on the general theme of 'Scientific Perspectives on Divine Action'. The founder and Director is Prof. Dr Robert John Russell.
Website: <http://www.ctns.org>

Centre for Science and Religion
This is an interdisciplinary centre at the University of Leeds (UK), founded in 1997. It covers the whole range of the sciences and many religious traditions – not just Christianity but also Islam, Judaism, Hinduism and Sikhism. It offers a complete taught MA in the area of science and religion. Directors: Dr Jacqui Stewart and Prof. Geoffrey Cantor.
Email: J.A.Stewart@leeds.ac.uk

Chicago Center for Religion and Science (CCRS)
CCRS is a programme arm of the Lutheran School of Theology at Chicago, operating in collaboration with the Center for Advanced Study in Religion and Science. It was founded in January 1988. The Center is dedicated to relating religious traditions and scientific knowledge in order to gain insight into the origins, nature, and future of humans and their environment, and to realize the common goal of a world in which love, justice, and ecologically responsible styles of living prevail. CCRS publishes the journal *Zygon*. Director: Prof. Dr Philip Hefner.
Website: <http://www.usao.edu/~facshaferi/CCRS.html>

The European Society for the Study of Science and Theology (ESSSAT)
ESSSAT is a scholarly, non-confessional organization (although it regards itself as committed to the Judaeo–Christian tradition), based in Europe. The Society aims to promote the study of relationships between the natural sciences and theological views. ESSSAT has members from almost every European country as well as members from other continents. They have different confessional backgrounds, and include believers as well as non-believers and atheists. As scientists, theologians, philosophers and historians they work on a better understanding of the interactions between religion and science. Every other year ESSSAT organizes a conference on a specific topic. The most important contributions to these conferences are published in the series Studies in Science & Theology (=SSTH). Members of ESSSAT receive the journal Science & Spirit. President: Prof. Dr Ulf Görman (Lund, Sweden); Secretary: Dr Antje Jackelen (Lund, Sweden).
Website: <http://www.ESSSAT.org>

The Heyendaal Centre for Theology and Science (HCTS)
HCTS is a section of the Heyendaal Institute, Nijmegen (Interdisciplinary Institute for Theology, Sciences and Culture) of the Catholic University of Nijmegen, the Netherlands. HCTS focuses on the relationship between theology on the one hand and the natural sciences, mathematics and computer sciences on the other. HCTS started on January 1999. Its first research program is focused on 'Self-organization as a scientific paradigm and the theological reflection on man and world'. The Director of the HCTS is Dr. Palmyre M.F. Oomen; the General Director of the Heyendaal Institute, Nijmegen, is Prof. Dr Hermann Häring.
E-mail: p.oomen@theo.kun.nl

Institute of Religion in an Age of Science
IRAS is a non-denominational, independent membership organization which has been working for a dynamic and positive relationship between religion and science since 1954. IRAS is an interdisciplinary group of scientists, theologians and others who are interested in exploring how to make religion more meaningful in a civilization dominated by sciences and their technologies. It has more than 300 members, widely distributed geographically, with international representation. IRAS is co-publisher of the quarterly journal *Zygon*, and membership in IRAS includes a subscription to *Zygon*. President: Dr Ursula Goodenough.
Website: <http://www.iras.org>

Institute for Theological Encounter with Science and Technology (ITEST)
ITEST is an international, interdisciplinary, interfaith community of Christians concerned with the revolutionary advance in scientific and technological capability, particularly as it is being directed toward living systems. ITEST involves over 600 members in 30 countries. It is an organization committed to ongoing dialogue among contemporary thinkers, assessing developments in science and technology

for their theological implications and to apply religious values to scientific processes. Director: Dr Robert A. Brungs, SJ.
Website: <http://itest.slu.edu>

The John Templeton Foundation
This Foundation is a non-profit grant-making organization, established in 1987 by Sir John Templeton. Its mission is to encourage the link between the sciences and all religions, to encourage a fresh appreciation of the critical importance of the moral and spiritual dimensions of life, and to explore spiritual and moral progress through the use of scientific methods. The John Templeton Foundation works closely with scientists, theologians, medical professionals, philosophers and scholars. At the moment it is the world's most important grant-making and research-stimulating organization. The Foundation currently funds more than 150 projects, studies, award programs and publications world-wide. As mentioned above, the John Templeton Foundation also compiles and edits the comprehensive reference book *Who's Who in Theology and Science*.
Website: <http://www.templeton.org>

Karl-Heim-Gesellschaft
The Karl-Heim-Gesellschaft is a German society, founded in 1974, of approximately 80 members and 550 friends who promote the legacy of Karl Heim (1874–1958) and hence a Christian orientation within a scientific–technological world through publications, seminars, and lectures. Every year it presents a volume of the series *Denken und Glauben*. Director: Prof.Dr Hans Schwarz.
Address: Unter den Eichen 13, D-3504 Marburg, Germany.

Meta
Meta is an edited, refereed and public listing dedicated to promoting the constructive engagement of science and religion and to sharing information and perspectives among the diverse organizations and individuals involved in this interdisciplinary field. It provides, among other things, book reviews, conference announcements and discussions. Editor: Dr William Grassie.
Subscription via: <http://www.meta-list.org>

Science & Spirit
Science & Spirit magazine is an independent periodical of news and opinion about the field of science and religion. It is now published five times a year with support from the John Templeton Foundation. Its purpose is to promote understanding, enlightenment and exploration of the relationships between issues of science and spirituality. Editors: Kevin Sharpe, John Teske and Chris Floyd. Subscription via email: info@science-spirit.org; or via the website.
Website: <http://www.science-spirit.org>

The Vatican Observatory

This Observatory is one of the oldest astronomical research institutions in the world. It has its headquarters at the papal summer residence in Castel Gandolfo, Italy, outside Rome. Its dependent research centre, the Vatican Observatory Research Group (VORG), is hosted by Steward Observatory at the University of Arizona, Tucson, USA. There is intensive co-operation with the Center for Theology and the Natural Sciences (CTNS) in the interdisciplinary research programme on the general theme of 'Scientific Perspectives on Divine Action'.
Director: Dr George V. Coyne, SJ.
Website: <http://clavius.as.arizona.edu/vo>

Zygon, Journal of Religion and Science

Zygon is a quarterly journal which explores the relationship between religious beliefs and philosophies and the theories and findings of modern-day science in order to illuminate issues of human purpose and moral direction in contemporary life. Founding Editor: Ralph Wendell Burhoe. Editor (since 1990): Philip Hefner. Publishing Agent: Basil Blackwell, Cambridge, MA / Oxford, UK. Subscription via email: subscrip@blackwellpub.com.

Here is some introductory literature on 'theology and science' and 'religion and science':

Barbour, I. G., *Issues in Science and Religion*, Englewood Cliffs, NJ: Prentice-Hall and London: SCM Press 1966.

——, *Religion and Science: Historical and Contemporary Issues*, San Francisco: HarperSanFrancisco and London: SCM Press 1997.

Brooke, J. H., *Science and Religion: Some Historical Perspectives*, Cambridge University Press 1991.

Coyne, G. V., K. Schmitz-Moormann and C. Wassermann (eds), *Origins, Time and Complexity* (2 volumes), Geneva: Labor et Fides 1994 [=SSTh 1 and SSTh 2].

Dippel, C. J. and J. M. de Jong, *Geloof en natuurwetenschap* (Part I), The Hague: Boekencentrum 1966.

Dippel, C. J. et al., *Geloof en natuurwetenschap* (Part II), The Hague: Boekencentrum 1967.

Drees, W. B., *Beyond the Big Bang: Quantum Cosmologies and God*, La Salle, IL: Open Court 1990.

——, *Religion, Science, and Naturalism*, Cambridge: Cambridge University Press 1995.

Driessen, A. and A. Suarez (eds), *Mathematical Undecidability, Quantum Nonlocality and the Question of the Existence of God*, Dordrecht/Boston/London: Kluwer 1997.

Fuchs, G. and H. Kessler (eds), *Gott, der Kosmos und die Freiheit: Biologie, Philosophie und Theologie im Gespräch*, Würzburg: Echter Verlag 1996, 189–232.

Glauben und Denken [Jahrbücher der Karl-Heim-Gesellschaft], Frankfurt am Main: Peter Lang.

Gregersen, N. H., M. W. S. Parsons and C. Wassermann (eds), *The Concept of Nature in Science and Theology* (2 volumes), Geneva: Labor et Fides 1997 and 1998 [=SSTh 3 and SSTh 4].

Gregersen, N. H. and J. W. van Huyssteen (eds.), *Rethinking Theology and Science: Six Models for the Current Dialogue*, Grand Rapids, Michigan / Cambridge, UK: Eerdmans 1998.

Gregersen, N. H., U. Görman and C. Wassermann (eds.), *The Interplay Between Scientific and Theological Worldviews* (2 volumes), Geneva: Labor et Fides 1999 [=SSTh 5 and SSTh 6].

Henry, G. C. *Logos: Mathematics and Christian Theology*, Lewisburg: Bucknell University Press 1976.

Hübner, J. (ed.), *Der Dialog zwischen Theologie und Naturwissenschaft: ein bibliografischer Bericht*, Munich: Christian Kaiser Verlag 1987.

Huyssteen, J. W. van, *The Shaping of Rationality: Toward Interdisciplinarity in Theology and Science*, Grand Rapids, Michigan / Cambridge, UK: Eerdmans 1999.

McGrath, A. E., *Science & Religion: An Introduction*, Oxford, UK / Malden, MA: Blackwell 1999.

Moltmann, J., *God in Creation. An Ecological Doctrine of Creation,* London: SCM Press 1985.

Müller, A. M. K. and W. Pannenberg (eds), *Erwägungen zu einer Theologie der Natur*, Gütersloh: Gerd Mohn 1970.

Overhage, P. and K. Rahner, *Das Problem der Hominisation: Über den biologischen Ursprung des Menschen*, Freiburg etc.: Herder 1961.

Pannenberg, W., *Toward a Theology of Nature: Essays on Science and Faith*, Louisville, Kentucky: Westminster/John Knox 1993.

Peacocke, A. R., *Creation and the World of Science* Oxford: Clarendon Press 1979.

——, *God and the New Biology*, London: Dent and Sons 1986.

——, *Theology for a Scientific Age*, London: SCM Press 1993.

Polkinghorne, J., *Science and Creation*, London: SPCK 1988.

——, *Science and Providence: God's Interaction with the World*, London: SPCK 1989.

——, *Science and Theology: An Introduction*, Minneapolis, MN: Fortress Press 1998.

Richardson, W. M. and W. J. Wildman (eds), *Religion and Science: History, Method, Dialogue*, New York/London: Routledge 1996.

Russell, R. J., W. J. Stoeger and G. V. Coyne (eds), *Physics, Philosophy, and Theology: A Common Quest for Understanding*, Vatican: Vatican Observatory (distributed via University of Notre Dame Press) 1988.

Russell, R. J., N. Murphy and C. J. Isham (eds), *Quantum Cosmology and the Laws of Nature: Scientific Perspective on Divine Action*, Berkeley CA: CTNS / Vatican City State: Vatican Observatory 1993.

Russell, R. J., N. Murphy and A. R. Peacocke (eds), *Chaos and Complexity: Scientific Perspectives on Divine Action*, Berkeley CA: CTNS / Vatican City State: Vatican Observatory 1995.

Russell, R. J., W. R. Stoeger and F. J. Ayala (eds), *Evolutionary and Molecular Biology: Scientific Perspectives on Divine Action*, Berkeley CA: CTNS / Vatican City State: Vatican Observatory 1997.

Schmitz-Moormann, K. (ed.), *Schöpfung und Evolution: Neue Ansätze zum Dialog zwischen Naturwissenschaften und Theologie*, Düsseldorf: Patmos Verlag 1992.

Theisen, G., *Biblical Faith: An Evolutionary Approach,* London: SCM Press 1985

Who's Who in Theology and Science, compiled and edited by the John Templeton Foundation, New York: Continuum Publishing Company 1996.

Wildiers, M., *Wereldbeeld en teologie*, Antwerpen/Amsterdam: Standaard Wetenschappelijke Uitgeverij [2]1977.

Worthing, M. W., *God, Creation, and Contemporary Physics*, Minneapolis, MN: Fortress Press 1996.

Contributors

PETER BLOEMERS is Professor of Biochemistry at the Catholic University of Nijmegen. He was born in 1936 in Roden and studied chemistry at the University of Utrecht, where he gained his doctorate. After a spell at Harvard Medical School he came to Nijmegen, where he rose to his present position.

Address: Weezenhof 26–66. 6536 JC Nijmegen, The Netherlands.

HERMANN HÄRING was born in 1937 and studied theology in Munich and Tübingen; between 1969 and 1980 he worked at the Institute of Ecumenical Research in Tübingen; since 1980 he has been Professor of Dogmatic Theology at the Catholic University of Nijmegen. His books include *Kirche und Kerygma. Das Kirchenbild in der Bultmannschule*, 1972; *Die Macht des Bösen. Das Erbe Augustins*, 1979; *Zum Problem des Bösen in der Theologie*, 1985; *Das Böse in der Welt*, 1999. He was co-editor of the *Wörterbuch des Christentums*, 1988, and has written articles on ecclesiology and christology, notably in the *Tijdschrift voor Theologie*.

Address: Katholieke Universiteit, Faculteit der Godgeleerdheid, Erasmusgebouw, Erasmusplein I, 6525 HT Nijmegen, Netherlands.

GEORGES DE SCHRIJVER was born in Belgium in 1935. He became a Jesuit in 1954 and then studied philosophy in Munich, Brussels and Leuven, and theology in Leuven and Paris. Since 1974 he has taught in the Catholic University of Leuven, where he is now a professor of religion. Since 1987 he has also been director of the centre for liberation theology there.

Address: Heilige-Geeeststraat 74/6, B 3000 Leuven, Belgium.

WILLEM B. DREES is a physicist, theologian and philosopher. He works at the Free University of Amsterdam and is Professor of the Philosophy of

Nature and Technology from a liberal Protestant perspective at the University of Twente. He is active in ESSSAT (European Society for the Study of Science and Theology), editor of ESSSAT News (1991–1998) and co-editor of the yearbooks (as of 1999). His publications include *Religion, Science and Naturalism,* Cambridge 1996; *Beyond the Big Bang: Quantum Cosmologies and God*, La Salle 1992 *and De mens: Meer dan materie? Religie en reductionisme*, Kampen, 1997.

Address: Bezinningscentrum VU, De Boelelaan 1105, NL, 1081 HV Amsterdam, The Netherlands.

Marjorie H. Suchocki gained her doctorate at Claremont Graduate School and from 1977 to 1983 was Professor of Theology at Pittsburgh Theological Seminary. From 1983 to 1990 she was Academic Dean and Professor of Systematic Theology, Wesley Theological Seminary, Washington, DC, and from 1993 to 1999 Vice President of Academic Affairs and Dean, Claremont School of Theology. She is currently Ingraham Professor of Theology, Claremont School of Theology and Professor of Religion, Claremont Graduate School. Her books include: *God – Christ – Church: A Practical Guide to Process Theology*, New York 1982, reissued 1995; The *Fall to Violence: Original Sin in Relational Theology*, New York 1994; *The Whispered Word: A Process Theology of Preaching,* St Louis 1999.

Address: Claremont School of Theology, 1325 North College Avenue, Claremont, CA 91711-3199, USA.

Christoph Theobald was born in Cologne in 1946 and became a Jesuit in the Province of France in 1978. He is Professor of Fundamental and Dogmatic Theology in the Theological Faculty of the Centre Sèvres, Paris, and editor of *Recherches de Science Religieuse,* to which he contributes a bulletin on systematic theology (God – Trinity). His works in the history of modern theology and systematic theology include *Maurice Blondel und das Problem der Modernität. Beitrag zu einer epistemologischen Standortbestimmung zeitgenössischer Fundamenaltheologie,* Frankfurt 1988, and 'La foi trinitaire des chrétiens et l'énigme du lien social. Contribution au debat sur la "théologie politique"', in *Monothéisme et Trinité,* Brussels 1991.

Address; 15, rue Monsieur, 75007 Paris, France.

BERNARD MICHOLLET was born in 1958. At university he had a basically scientific training (in mathematics and physics). He is assistant at the faculty of theology at the University of Lyons and is working on the question of relationships between the sciences and theology. His current thesis is on the cognitive sciences and theology. Articles include 'De l'intelligence artificielle au souffle de Dieu', in *La peau de l'âme,* ed. Michel Simon, Paris 1995, and 'The Interest of Neurobiology for Theological Anthropology', *Studies in Science and Theology*, 1997.

Address: 7 place Saint Irénée, 69005 Lyon, France.

ANTONY F. CAMPBELL is a New Zealander by birth, a Jesuit in Australia by conviction, and a student of the Older Testament by passion. He studied Greek, history and biblical archaeology at the University of Melbourne, theology at Lyons, France and scripture at the Pontifical Biblical Institute in Rome and at Claremont Graduate School, California. He has a DD from the Melbourne College of Divinity. He has been teaching the Older Testament at Jesuit Theological College, within the United Faculty of Theology, Melbourne, since his return to Australia in 1974. His books include: *The Ark Narrative (1 Sam. 4–6; 2 Sam.* 6). Missoula, Montana 1975; *Of Prophets and Kings: A Late Ninth-Century Document (I Samuel 1–2 Kings 10)*. Washington, DC 1986; *The Study Companion to Old Testament Literature,* Collegeville, MN 1989/1992; and *Sources of the Pentateuch: Texts, Introductions, Annotations,* with Mark A. O'Brien, Minneapolis 1993.

Address: Jesuit Theological College, 175 Royal Parade, Parkville, Victoria 3052, Australia.

LODOVICO GALLENI was born in Pisa in 1947. He teaches zoology at the University of Pisa and science and theology at the Higher Institute of Religious Sciences, also in Pisa, and at the Inter-Diocesan Theological Study Centre in Lucca. He is co-ordinator of the biological section of the international research project into the foundations of science at the Pontifical Lateran University and a member of the executive council of the European Society for the Study of Science and Theology. He also belongs to the editorial committee of the journals *Studies in Science* and *Theology and Biology* Forum. His books include: *Scienza e Teologia, proposte per una sintesi feconda*, Brescia 1992 and *Da Darwin a Teilhard de Chardin, interventi sull'evolutione*, Pisa 1996.

Address: Via Vettori 15, I 56127, Pisa, Italy.

THOMAS AYKARA is professor at Dharamram Vidya Kshetram, Pontifical Athenaeum of Philosophy and Theology in Bangalore, India. He has been teaching mainly philosophical anthropology, theological anthropology and comparative religion for about three decades. He took his PhD in philosophy at the Catholic University of Leuven and his DPhil. in theology and comparative religion at the University of Oxford. He is the author of *Cosmic Consciousness. A Comparative Study on Teilhard de Chardin and Sri Aurobindo*, and the editor of *Meeting of Religions, Missiology for the Third Millennium.* He is on the editorial board of the international quarterlies *Journal of Dharma* and *Third Millennium.*

Address: Centre for Indian and Inter-Religious Studies, Corso Vittorio Emanuele 294/10, 00186 Rome, Italy.

PALMYRE M. F. OOMEN was born in Breda, The Netherlands, in 1948 and studied philosophy and biology in Leiden and Delft, and theology and philosophy in Nijmegen. She gained her doctorate on an interpretation of Whitehead's philosophy and the agency of God (*Doet God ertoe? Een interpretatie van Whitehead als bijdrage aan een theologie van Gods handelen*, Kampen: Kok,1998). She has written a number of articles on the relationship between theology and science and is Director of the Heyendaal Center for Theology and Science (HCTS) of the Heyendaal Institute (University of Nijmegen).

Address: Okapistraat 56, 6531 RM Nijmegen, the Netherlands.
Email: p.oomen@theo.kun.nl

The editors wish to thank the great number of colleagues who contributed in a most helpful way to the final project of this issue.

J. Alemany	Madrid	Spain
M. Althaus-Reid	Edinburgh	Scotland
N. Ančič	Split	Croatia
J. Argüello	Managua	Nicaragua
J. Arnould	Paris	France
O. Beozzo	São Paulo	Brazil
T. Berger	North Carolina	USA
L. Sowle Cahill	Chestnut Hill	America
P. F. Carneiro de Andrade	Rio de Janeiro	Brazil
C. Carozzo	Genoa	Italy
J. Coleman	Los Angeles	USA
R. Cote	Ontario	Canada
L. A. de Boni	Porte Alegre	Brazil
K. Derksen	Utrecht	The Netherlands
K. Egan	Indiana	USA
F. Elizondo	Madrid	Spain
R. Gibellini	Brescia	Italy
E. Green	Bari	Italy
M. Grey	Wiltshire	England
O. John	Ibbenbüren	Germany
B. Kern	Mainz	Germany
U. King	Bristol	England
K.-J. Kuschel	Tübingen	Germany
H. Lepargneur	São Paulo	Brazil
S. McEvenue	Montreal	Canada
J. de Mesa	Manila	Philippines
N. Mette	Münster	Germany
J.-B. Metz	Münster	Germany
J.-G. Nadeau	Montreal	Canada
M. O'Brien	Box Hill	Australia
S. Painadath	Kerala	India
P. Philibert	Notre Dame	USA
A. Pieris	Kelaniya	Sri Lanka
M. Pilar Aquino	San Diego	USA
M. Purwatma	Yogyakarta	Indonesia
J. Riches	Glasgow	Scotland
G. Ruggieri	Catania	Italy
R. Schotsmans	Leuven	Belgium
R. Schreiter	Chicago	America
S. Schroer	Köniz	Switzerland
D. Singles	Lyon	France
J. Walsh	Gaborone	Botswana
F. Wilfred	Madras	India

CONCILIUM

Concilium: Subscription Information

Issues to be published in 2000

February 2000/1: *Evolution and Faith*
edited by Hermann Häring and Christoph Theobald

April 2000/2: *Creating Identity*
edited by Hermann Häring, Maureen Junker-Kenny and Dietmar Mieth

June 2000/3: *Religion During and After Communism*
edited by Miklós Tomka and Paul M. Zulehner

October 2000/4: *The Bright Side of Faith*
edited by Elsa Tamez and Ellen van Wolde

December 2000/5: *In the Power of Wisdom*
edited by Maria Pilar Aquino and Elisabeth Schüssler Fiorenza

---

To receive *Concilium 2000* (five issues) **anywhere in the world**, please copy this form, complete it in block capitals and send it with your payment to:

SCM Press *(Concilium)* 9–17 St Albans Place London N1 0NX England
Telephone (44) 20 7359 8033 Fax (44) 20 7359 0049

☐ Individual **£25.00**/*US$50.00* ☐ Institutional **£35.00**/*US$75.00*

Issues are sent by air to the USA; please add £10/US$20 for airmail dispatch to all other countries (outside Europe).

☐ I enclose a cheque payable to SCM–Canterbury Press Ltd for £/$ ....

☐ Please charge my MasterCard/Visa Expires ....

\# ..../........................../.........................../..........................

Signature ....

Name/Institution ....

Address ....

....

....

Telephone ....Fax ....

E-mail ....